Walking in the Spirit
A Fruitful Life

Walking in the Spirit
A Fruitful Life

by
Sharon Daugherty

HARRISON HOUSE
Tulsa, Oklahoma

Cover photo by Scott Collins.

2nd Printing
Over 15,000 in Print

*Walking in the Spirit —
A Fruitful Life*
ISBN 0-89274-502-9
Copyright © 1984 by Sharon Daugherty
Victory Christian Center
7700 S. Lewis
Tulsa, OK 74136

Published by Harrison House, Inc.
P. O. Box 35035
Tulsa, Oklahoma 74153

TABLE OF CONTENTS

WALKING IN THE SPIRIT — A Fruitful Life

Foreword

"This I say then, Walk in the Spirit, and ye shall not fulfill the lust of the flesh...the fruit of the Spirit is love, joy, peace, longsuffering, gentleness, goodness, faith, meekness, temperance: against such there is no law" (Galatians 5:16,22,23).

The first impression that usually comes to mind when we think of someone who "walks in the Spirit" is a person who knows the Bible well, has a distant, quiet personality, and operates in the supernatural gifts of the Spirit listed in 1 Corinthians 12. However, this is not the description of walking in the Spirit which Galatians 5 gives to us.

"Walking in the Spirit" is simply not walking by the dictates of the flesh, but instead, being controlled by the Spirit within. When you received Jesus into your heart, you received His fullness. His nature came to live and abide in you. Your old way of life ceased to exist, and a new life began. You received the Spirit of God into your heart.

"Walking in the Spirit" is to walk according to the lifestyle of Jesus, who is now in you. Galatians 5:23 describes this lifestyle as one of love, joy, peace, longsuffering, gentleness, goodness, faith, meekness, and temperance. You might think that walking in the fruit of the Spirit is difficult and unattainable, but it really isn't. Once you understand that it isn't you living your life any more but Jesus, then you begin to allow Jesus to flow through you.

You begin to live in the Spirit the moment you are born again. You become a living spirit, alive unto God and dead to the old life. Your state of being is then "in Christ." *"Therefore if any man be **in Christ,** he is a new creature: old things are passed away; behold, all things are become new"* (2 Corinthians 5:17). But living in the Spirit and walking in the Spirit are two different things.

I have known children who were born into a family and lived as a part of a family but did not walk (or conduct) themselves like the parents or the rest of the family. You can be born into God's family and even live in God's family but not walk like our Father. Another example is a small baby who is definitely alive but has not made the effort to *walk* yet. Babies have been born into the kingdom of God who are definitely alive unto God but are not walking like their Father God. *"Whoever says he abides in Him ought—as a personal debt—to walk and conduct himself in the same way in which He walked and conducted Himself"* (1 John 2:6, AMPLIFIED).

When you are born again, you receive a brand new nature on the inside—the very nature of God Himself! The characteristics of His nature—love, joy, peace, longsuffering, gentleness, goodness, faithfulness, meekness, and self-control—are implanted within your spirit when you are born again. The growth process of these characteristics is then

6

ready to begin in your soul and body realms.

If you walk in the Spirit and are led by the Spirit of God, you will be able to live the richest, most abundant life available to mankind—to live in Christ Jesus and to walk as He walked. And the fruit of His Spirit will flourish in and through you. You will notice that increasingly you will have no desire to gratify your flesh, for you will submit your flesh to your born-again spirit, which is now dominated by the Holy Spirit of God.

To be led by the flesh is to manifest the fruit of the flesh. *"...immorality, impurity, indecency, idolatry, sorcery, enmity, strife, jealousy, anger (ill temper), selfishness, divisions (dissensions), party spirit (factions, sects, with peculiar opinions, heresies), envy, drunkenness, carousing, and the like..."* (Galatians 5:19-21, AMPLIFIED). In verse 21, Paul continues, *"...I warn you beforehand, just as I did previously, that those who do such things shall not inherit the kingdom of God."* But to be led of the Spirit is to manifest the fruit of the Spirit—love, joy, peace, longsuffering, gentleness, goodness, faith, meekness, and temperance.

Sometimes Christians who desire to walk in the Spirit with the fruit of the Spirit blossoming in their lives don't seem to have any control over the lusts of the flesh. Modern believers aren't the only ones who have experienced this problem. Paul recognized this same conflict within himself. He wrote *"I descern in my bodily members—in the sensitive appetites and wills of the flesh—a different law (rule of action) at war against the law of my mind (my reason) and making me a prisoner of the law of sin that dwells*

7

in my bodily organs—in the sensitive appetites and wills of the flesh" (Romans 7:23, AMPLIFIED).

Paul goes on to say that one of the keys to walking in the Spirit is *to set your mind upon the things of the Spirit. "To be carnally minded is death; to be spiritually minded is life and peace"* (Romans 8:6). I find that the more I set my mind on God's Word, the more I live in abundant life and in the peace of God. Where there is a lack of God's Word, there will be a lack of abundant life and peace.

Second Peter 1:4 says that we've been given the Word of God to partake of the divine nature of Jesus and to escape the corruption that's in the world through lust. It is by getting God's Word into your heart and mind that you *will be able to escape the lusts of the flesh* and be able to confidently walk in the Spirit.

It will take conscious effort on your part to determine *to walk in the Spirit* and exemplify God's fruit. Once you have made that decision, perhaps your next question is, *"How* do I walk in the Spirit and bring forth the new nature that is within me on the outside?"

In the following pages, we will discuss each fruit of the Spirit and how to walk out or exemplify the life of Jesus.

The deeper your revelation is of Jesus through the Word and through prayer, the greater will be the manifestation of His fruit in your life! And evidence of His fruit will truly indicate that you are not only living in the Spirit but that you are also WALKING IN THE SPIRIT!

Sharon Daugherty

1
The Growth Process

A scientist once said that thorns on rose bushes are actually undeveloped roses. I feel almost certain that in the beginning, when God created the earth, there were no thorns on rose bushes. I personally feel that the thorns came after Adam and Eve sinned.

We can see the analogy of the rose bush in the Christian kingdom. While many Christians go through the growth process and develop into beautiful roses, some do not and become thorns in the Body of Christ, always sticking and hurting people if they are touched wrongly or having to be dealt with a certain way so they won't get upset and hurt another person. So we can see how vital the growth process of the Christian really is!

Learning to walk in the Spirit requires a process of time. It will not occur within a day or even within a month, even though all nine fruit of the Spirit of God were implanted within you as "seed" when you were born again. *"Being born again, not of corruptible seed, but of incorruptible, by the word of God, which liveth and abideth for ever"* (1 Peter 1:23). As the diagram on the following page shows, there are several stages of the seed's growth. In this chapter we will discuss these growth stages:

1. The seed.
2. The tender sprout.
3. The young seedling.

4. The tree with leaves.
5. The tree with blossoms.
6. The tree with fruit.

You must nurture the seed daily for it to germinate. If you do not nurture it, it will become stagnant (dull, motionless, or inactive). In the same way, we must nurture the seed of God's Word in our lives so that it will grow.

The Word of God—which is the seed— is first solidly planted in the good soil of your heart when you receive Jesus. As the seed begins to grow, your roots must extend deep into the soil, establishing your heart. *"As ye have therefore received Christ Jesus the Lord,* **so walk ye in him: Rooted** *and* **built up** *in him and* **stablished** *in the faith, as ye have been taught, abounding therein with thanksgiving"* (Colossians 2:6,7)

The Japanese cultivate exquisite miniature trees called bonsai trees. Although perfectly proportioned, their total size is dwarfed by deliberately clipping their roots. Because of this special clipping, these trees will never grow to their full size, even though they are mature in every other way.

God doesn't want your roots to be cut or dwarfed. He wants *your* roots to go down deep into the soil of His Word and to spring forth in the length and the height and the depth of His love so that you may grow into the fullness of maturity in Jesus.

"For he shall be like a tree planted by the waters, that spreads out its roots by the river, and shall not see and fear when heat comes, but his leaf shall be green; he shall not be anxious and careful in the year of drought, nor shall

he cease from yielding fruit" (Jeremiah 17:8, AMPLIFIED).

The seed, through nourishment from the Word of God, germinates into the first stage of growth and brings forth a young, tender sprout. The young seedling can be easily bruised, injured, or hindered if it is not properly cared for and nourished. Jesus takes tender care with the newborn Christian, as a small weak reed. *"A bruised reed He will not break, and a smoldering (dimly burning) wick He will not quench..."* (Matthew 12:20). *The Living Bible* says, *"He does not crush the weak, or quench the smallest hope...."* Jesus understands where we are in our growth and extends His grace to us when we are weak. He seems to take joy in showing Himself strong when we are weak and have exhausted our own natural strength. A reminder to Christians is that just as Jesus is tender and forbearing with us, we must be tender and forbearing with one another throughout the various stages of Christian growth.

The seedling will mature into a young tree as it is affectionately cared for and properly nourished. Its roots will extend deep into the soil. This is parallel to the growth of a Christian. As he receives *daily* nourishment from the Word of God, affectionate care from the Body of Christ, and regular teaching of truths of God's Word, the Christian's roots will grow deep into the Father God.

The depth of the Christian's roots refers not only to a knowledge of the Word, but also to an understanding of it, enabling him to become a *doer* of the Word. *"But be ye doers of the word, and not hearers only, deceiving your own selves"* (James 1:22)

As the leaves spring forth upon the young tree, they are pretty and they provide shade, but they cannot be eaten for nourishment or for any other reason. You, as a child of God, must go on to perfection (maturity) if you are to be mightily used of God in providing His nourishment and truths to others. In Mark 11, Jesus looked for fruit on a fig tree that had many pretty leaves. It was deceptive, because from a distance it looked like it should be full of fruit, but when Jesus got close to it, it had no fruit.

Jesus is looking for fruit in our lives. He doesn't want us to look fruitful from a distance but be barren when one actually gets a closer look at us. We must go on to maturity and grow in Him.

As the young tree matures, blossoms will come forth. The blossoms are always beautiful, and they will give off a fragrance, attracting the attention of others. So will it be in your life as a Christian. Your blossoms will cause others to be drawn to the sweet aroma of Christ! *"Now thanks be unto God, which always causeth us to triumph in Christ, and maketh manifest the savour of his knowledge by us in every place. For we are unto God a sweet savour of Christ, in them that are saved, and in them that perish"* (2 Corinthians 2:14,15).

Blossoms indicate that fruit will soon be forthcoming. Tiny fruit begins to protrude through the blossoms. Finally the blossoms totally disappear, but the fruit remains. Although the fruit may begin small, in a process of time, it will become large and luscious. As the fruit becomes mature for eating, people will partake of it with much enjoyment.

Likewise, as the fruit of God's Spirit matures within you, His precious child, people will seek you out for wisdom and counsel, partaking of your love, joy, and peace.

Factors in Growth

There are several other factors in the Christian's growth which you need to recognize, particularly the factors of soil, water, light, and season (or timing).

Soil

We mentioned earlier that your heart must be good soil to receive God's Word, the nutrient used to germinate the seeds of God's nature implanted within you when you are born again.

When you are first born again, you will hunger for the Word of God. After a season, however, sometimes because of the pressures and cares of daily life and a lack of time spent in the presence of the Lord, some Christians have slacked off in their desire for God's Word and have allowed their hearts to become hardened. We must never allow ourselves to become too hardened for the Spirit to move in. The Scriptures say we must "stir" ourselves so as not to get this way.

We need to purpose in our hearts, as an act of our own will, to seek the Lord daily through His Word, through prayer, through fellowship, and through special time spent in quiet before Him that we might grow thereby. The Word of God says, *"Sow to yourselves righteousness, reap the fruit of unfailing love, and break up the unplowed ground; for it is time to seek the Lord, until he comes and showers righteousness on you"* (Hosea 10:12, NIV).

Another necessary ingredient for growth—water—will help keep the ground of your heart soft and pliable in God's hands.

Water

The water of God's Word and His Spirit are essential ingredients for the Christian's growth. Water is an emblem of the Holy Spirit and the Word of God.

You must seek the Lord for the rains of the Spirit to fall in your life, refreshing the soil of your heart and stimulating your spirit. *"Ask ye of the Lord rain in the time of the latter rain; so the Lord shall make bright clouds, and give them showers of rain, to every one grass in the field"* (Zechariah 10:1).

God says that there must be a repentant heart before the water or times of refreshing will come to your spirit. *"So repent—change your mind and purpose; turn around and return [to God], that your sins may be erased (blotted out, wiped clean), that times of refreshing—of recovering from the effects of heat, of reviving with fresh air— may come from the presence of the Lord"* (Acts 3:19, AMPLIFIED).

God's refreshing and rest also come through praying in the Spirit. *"For with stammering lips and another tongue will he speak to this people. To whom he said, This is the rest wherewith ye may cause the weary to rest: and this is the refreshing..."* (Isaiah 28:11,12).

Worshipping the Lord brings us the rain of His Spirit.

I'm not speaking of just singing some songs in a church service; I'm speaking of singing to the Lord during your day and praising Him for what He has done and for who He is. *"And it shall be, that **whoso** of the families of the earth **shall not go up** to Jerusalem **to worship** the King, the Lord of hosts, **upon them there shall be no rain"*** (Zechariah 14:17, AMPLIFIED). Zechariah went so far as to say that if a person refuses to worship the Lord, he will receive no rain.

God's Word also acts to cleanse and refresh us. Jesus Himself sanctifies and cleanses you with the washing of water by His Word. *"So that He might sanctify her, having cleansed her **by the washing of water with the Word"*** (Ephesians 5:26). As you study the Word of God and allow it to dwell in you richly, it will cleanse you and will stimulate growth in your life.

Isaiah 55:10-11 says, *"For **as the rain and snow come down** from the heavens, and return not there again, but water the earth and make it bring forth and sprout, that it may give seed to the sower and bread to the eater, **so shall My word be that goes forth out of My mouth; it shall not return to Me void—without producing any effect, useless—but it shall accomplish that which I please and purpose, and it shall prosper in the thing for which I sent it"*** (AMPLIFIED).

Continually allow God's Spirit and His Word to water the seeds of His nature planted within your heart that you might become a flourishing branch of the wholesome Vine, Jesus Christ!

Light

Plants (or seeds) must have light to cause them to flourish in abundant vitality. Likewise, the Christian must have light in the Word of God and in fellowship with other Christians to flourish in a stable walk in Christ Jesus.

New Christians often desire to witness of their new-found life in Christ to their former friends who are still in darkness. Although it is important to witness to those in darkness (in Satan's domain), it is essential that you discontinue your close fellowship with those who are still in darkness. *"Be ye not unequally yoked together with unbelievers: for what fellowship hath righteousness with unrighteousness? and what communion hath light with darkness?"* (2 Corinthians 6:14).

You must remember that as a newborn baby, you are still weak and the devil would try to tempt you in your weak areas. You can share with people without going and fellowshipping with them in their darkness. Proverbs 13:20 says, *"He that walketh with wise men shall be wise: but a companion of fools shall be destroyed."*

Continued fellowship with those in darkness has caused many a new convert to fall by the wayside. Ask the Lord for new Christian friends who will be able to help you grow. Then after more growth, you'll be stronger spiritually and will be able to be around unbelievers and bring them to the Lord without their pulling you down.

To walk in the light, we must seek the light of God's Word. *"Thy word is a lamp unto my feet, and a light unto my path"* (Psalm 119:105). *"The entrance of thy words giveth light; it giveth understanding unto the simple"* (Psalm 119:130).

As you study God's Word, it will bring you light and make you aware of His plan and purpose for your life, because He has a unique, divine plan for you. Don't settle for unclear direction. Seek God's Word for His plan for you. Ask Him to enlighten your understanding that His plan for you may become crystal clear.

"[For I always pray] the God of our Lord Jesus Christ, the Father of Glory, that He may grant you a spirit of wisdom and revelation—of insight into mysteries and secrets—in the [deep and intimate] knowledge of Him, by **having the eyes of your heart flooded with light, so that you can know and understand the hope to which He has called you** *and how rich is His glorious inheritance in the saints—His set-apart ones"* (Ephesians 1:17,18, AMPLIFIED).

Time

Time or "due season" is also essential to the fulfillment of maturity of fruit, both in nature and in the Christian's life. Ecclesiastes 3:11 says that God makes all things beautiful in **His** time. You must remember that a seed does not become a tree overnight. Everything that lives takes time to grow and mature. Even after much growth we need time for seasoning or ripening.

I recall one time when my husband and I had just returned home from a ministry trip. I went to the grocery store to stock up on a few items, and I saw a specially priced batch of bananas. I selected some which looked perfect—

ones totally free of spots and bruises, although they were slightly green. When I got home, I decided to try one of the perfect bananas. I had to get a knife to pry the peel open. I could hardly separate the peel from the banana. It was quite obvious that the banana needed more time to ripen to full maturity.

That's the way it is with Christians. We don't become mature the moment we are born again. Maturity will surely come, but it will take a process of time. Keep pressing on **toward** maturity, yet remain in peace and rest during this season of growth. *"Let us therefore be zealous and exert ourselves and strive diligently to enter into the rest..."* (Hebrews 4:11, AMPLIFIED).

Desire to be content at each stage of your growth in the Lord, pressing upward and onward daily "in Him." However, do not be so satisfied with the growth you have attained thus far that you don't desire to grow any more. My husband has often said that perfection can be attained at each stage of growth for a person—it's not just a goal at the end of life. *"But grow in grace (undeserved favor, spiritual strength) and recognition and knowledge and understanding of our Lord and Saviour Jesus Christ, the Messiah..."* (2 Peter 3:18, AMPLIFIED).

2
Love

The word "love" is excessively overused in our society, expressing an attitude about anything from people to foods to clothes to pets or other things. Fortunately, the Greeks are more specific in their definition and use of the word "love." The three kinds of love which we will discuss are agape, phileo, and eros.

When you are born again, you receive the God-kind of love—*AGAPE*—into your heart. In fact, our salvation is proved by our love for other brothers and sisters in the Lord. This God-kind of love promotes a kindred bond between Christians. *"We know that we have passed over out of death into the Life by the fact that we love the brethren [our fellow Christians]..."* (1 John 3:14, AMPLIFIED).

However, this love is much more than a kindredship between Christians; it is a selfless love, willing to deny itself for the benefit of the other person. This love will go so far as dying for its enemies. *"But God commendeth his love toward us, in that, while we were yet sinners, Christ died for us"* (Romans 5:8).

Vine relates it this way: "Christian love has God for its primary object, and expresses itself first of all in implicit obedience to His commandments. This love *is not an impulse from the feelings, it does not always run with the natural inclinations, nor does it spend itself only upon those for whom some affinity is discovered. Love can be* known only from the actions it prompts." *Agape* love is based upon a quality decision, a deliberate choice—not on a feeling.

The world seems to be most familiar with *EROS* love, which refers to physical love, usually governed by the five senses. From *eros* is derived the word "erotic," which is a sensual love.

Many relationships start out on the *EROS* level (physical love) when a man and woman are physically attracted to each other. Their attempt to grow closer to one another may eventually end up in sin. If this happens, their hearts will become hardened toward God and the things of God as well as each other! This is because *eros* love is based on gratifying self, so when self is not fulfilled, it ends.

PHILEO describes brotherly love or human love. This kind of love can be very strong, but under pressure it can stop. Some people have operated in this kind of love without even knowing God and have given their lives for others because of it. You probably have heard of men who, during times of war, have given their lives for fellow soldiers and for their country. But *phileo* is based on feelings. When one is operating solely in *phileo* love, he can give love only to a person he has some feeling or affinity for.

Relationships built upon *phileo* or human love often are terminated when arguments arise. Sometimes in marriage this stormy type of relationship survives long enough to bring a form of religion into the picture, but such a relationship often ends in divorce because the foundation of human love is not solid.

When a couple starts their relationship with *AGAPE*, the God-kind of love—unselfish love—they will be willing to give up their own selfish desires for the benefit of the other person. They will keep their physical attraction under control. (Self-control is also a fruit of the Spirit).

Agape love has self-control. *Eros* love says, "I can't wait," but *agape* love says, "I can wait." *Agape* love is patient, because it sees a more beautiful way of fulfillment for both people. A good marriage is first based on *agape* love, then *phileo* and *eros*.

Agape love is God's highest and most fulfilling plan for every person, whether in a marriage relationship or in our daily relationships with all people.

God's plan is that *AGAPE* always be in control of your life, leading and directing you, spilling over into every area of your life.

Agape Love

The best definition the Bible gives us for *agape* love is found in 1 Corinthians 13:4-8, AMPLIFIED:

> *"Love endures long and is patient and kind; love never is envious nor boils over with jealousy; is not boastful or vainglorious, does not display itself haughtily.*

> *"It is not conceited—arrogant and inflated with pride; it is not rude (unmannerly), and does not act unbecomingly. Love [God's love in us] does not*

insist on its own rights or its own way, for it is not self-seeking; it is not touchy or fretful or resentful; it takes no account of the evil done to it— pays no attention to a suffered wrong.

"It does not rejoice at injustice and unrighteousness, but rejoices when right and truth prevail.

"Love bears up under anything and everything that comes, is ever ready to believe the best of every person, its hopes are fadeless under all circumstances and it endures everything [without weakening].

"Love never fails—never fades out or becomes obsolete or comes to an end...."

Love is Patient

God is *"...longsuffering (extraordinarily patient) toward you, not desiring that any should perish, but that all should turn to repentance"* (2 Peter 3:9, AMPLIFIED).

God is so loving that He is waiting for great multitudes to come into the kingdom before Jesus returns for His glorious church.

If we are to become like Jesus, to be led by the Holy Spirit, to walk "in Christ Jesus," and to abide in Him, then we must seek to become as patient as He. God never gives up on people, so neither can we!

When working as youth pastors, my husband and I were challenged to exhibit patient love on several occasions. Some young boys came to youth meetings only to create disturbances with their rowdy, rebellious behavior. We needed the wisdom of God to handle such situations. As we continued in steadfast, patient love, mixed with faith in God's Word, we saw the day when all of these boys received Jesus as their Lord and Saviour.

I also have found that patient love is necessary in a marriage relationship. My husband and I realized that it would take a joint effort to have a good marriage relationship. We were two distinct individuals having two separate minds and two separate backgrounds which had to be melted and molded into one.

I was a person who could barely make appointments on time, while my husband was always prompt to keep appointments. In a loving way we discussed how he could be of help to me and how I could better plan, meeting all of my schedules and deadlines. Then we prayed together. Billy Joe has had to be very patient with me at times, but God has helped me triumph in this area. Even when there have been times when I failed to be punctual, my husband has covered me with his love.

"Above all things have intense and unfailing love for one another, for love covers a multitude of sins—forgives and disregards the offenses of others" (I Peter 4:8, AMPLIFIED). Praying in the Spirit enables us to love each other *past* our failures and to have patience with one another when necessary!

We in the Body of Christ must make every effort to walk in patience and love to cover the faults of others. Praying at these times will help us overcome.

Love is Kind

You need to be considerate of situations and people, preferring the other person before yourself. Paul exhorted us with this thought in Ephesians 4:32, *"And become useful and helpful and kind to one another, tenderhearted (compassionate, understanding, loving-hearted)..."* (AMPLIFIED).

Kindness is a quality that has almost been neglected in our generation because of the popular self-seeking attitudes which exist in society. This day of fast-paced living has subtly caused people to barely have time for themselves, much less for others.

The Word of God looks at people and situations quite differently. *"Let each of you esteem and look upon and be concerned for not [merely] his own interests, but also each for the interests of others"* (Philippians 2:4, AMPLIFIED).

Love sees a need and steps out to fill it. In Luke 10:30-37, Jesus told the parable of the Good Samaritan. In this story, the Good Samaritan performed a kindness to one who had been considered an enemy. This is a perfect illustration of one who saw a need and took time to step out to fulfill it because of the compassion of God within him. God's kindness is exemplified in our actions and not just our words. *"...faith without works is dead..."* (James 2:26).

Love is Not Envious

The God-kind of love is always filled with excitement

26

over the prosperity and well-being of others.

Never allow jealousy to enter into your heart or make you envious of another's position or prosperity. Keep a healthy, positive attitude toward others as they flourish in Christ Jesus. For as you continue to seek first the things of the Kingdom of God, He will add "all these things" unto your life (Matthew 6:33).

Love Is Not Boastful or Vainglorious, Is Not Puffed Up, Is Not Conceited

"For [it is] not [the man] who praises and commends himself who is approved and accepted, but [it is the person] whom the Lord accredits and commends" (2 Corinthians 10:18, AMPLIFIED).

One of my professors at Oral Roberts University who had succeeded in fulfilling his dreams once quoted the verse, *"If you are gifted and talented, your gift will make room for you"* (Proverbs 18:16).

You need to be willing to be used of the Lord, but do not promote yourself. A pushy spirit reveals conceit and pride rather than a godly character. Human nature prompts us to emphasize the fact that "I" laid hands on someone, and they were healed. Or "I" sang and people fell on their knees in repentance to God. Your emphasis must not be on the personal "I," but let God be the One who is magnified.

James 4:6 says, *"But He gives us more and more grace [power of the Holy Spirit, to meet this evil tendency and all others fully.] That is why He says, God sets Himself against the proud and haughty, but gives grace [continually] to the lowly—those who are humble-minded [enough to receive it]"* (AMPLIFIED). Grace means "divine favor," and God will give favor to the humble.

"Therefore humble yourselves (demote, lower yourselves in your own estimation) under the mighty hand of God, that in due time He may exalt you" (1 Peter 5:6, AMPLIFIED). There is a "due season" for your exaltation, but let it come from the Lord.

I grew up in small towns, and I had many opportunities to sing. I guess you could say that I was "a big fish in little ponds." But when I went to Oral Roberts University, there were many other talented people there. And God kept my singing opportunities to a minimum, because He wanted to teach me some more important lessons. God was doing an inner work to reveal His character in me. (Many times I felt like Moses in the days of his preparation in the desert before God really used him.)

When my husband and I were led into an evangelistic ministry and later into a pastorate, God began using the gift He had given me to a much greater degree. He has taught me, however, that I am *totally* dependent upon Him.

Humility is a *total* dependence upon God. Thinking and speaking in a degrading manner about yourself is not humility; it is actually a form of self-exaltation. Don't get caught in that trap! But remember who your Source is.

Avail yourself and let God exalt *you* in His time!

Love Doesn't Behave Itself Unbecomingly

Always attempt to be mannerly and gracious, seeking *never* to offend in word or deed, always considering the feelings of others.

Ecclesiastes 3:1 says, *"To every thing there is a season, and a time for every matter or purpose under heaven"* (AMPLIFIED).

There's a time to laugh and a time to cry; there's a time to be silent and a time to speak; there's a time to mourn and a time to dance...

Learn to be sensitive to the Spirit of God, and He will be your guide in every situation to act becomingly.

Love Doesn't Insist Upon Having Its Own Way

In John 5:30 Jesus said, *"I am able to do nothing from Myself—independently, of My own accord; but as I am taught by God and as I get His orders. [I decide as I am bidden to decide. As the voice comes to Me, so I give a decision.] Even as I hear, I judge and My judgment is right (just, righteous),* **because I do not seek or consult my own will—***I have no desire to do what is pleasing to Myself, My own aim, My own purpose—***but only the will and pleasure of the Father Who sent Me"** (AMPLIFIED).

Love seeks God's will, not self will; and Jesus Christ is the perfect example of selflessness for man to follow. In the Garden of Gethsemane, Jesus *"...threw Himself upon the ground on His face and prayed saying, My Father, if* *it is possible, let this cup pass away from Me; nevertheless, not what I will—not what I desire—**but as You will and desire***" (Matthew 26:39, AMPLIFIED).

In His humanness, Jesus did not want to go through the cross experience. But as the Son of God, He knew he *must* carry out God's plan. Jesus exemplified total selflessness, and in so doing, God gave Him a Name which is above all names—in heaven, on earth, and under the earth.

It is in self-denial that we keep an open channel for the divine flow of God's love to move through us, as is seen in Luke 9:23. *"And to all he said, If anyone wishes to be a follower of mine, he must leave self behind; day after day he must take up his cross, and come with me"* (NEW ENGLISH BIBLE).

Love Is Not Touchy, Resentful, or Easily Provoked

God has provided a way for you to stay in His love walk when people seem to rub you the wrong way. God's way to remain in love is similar to the old cliche—"like water off a duck's back." Ducks have small oil beads under their feathers, and they sometimes sit for an hour or more popping the oil beads with their beaks before they get into the water. That's how you need to be in the love walk!

Pop the oil beads of the Holy Spirit in your life through *prayer* and through *time in God's Word*. Then when people say things that would normally hurt or offend you, let it roll off you like water off a duck's back! *"Great peace have they which love thy law; and nothing shall offend*

30

them" (Psalm 119:165). If you set your heart and mind to think on things which are true, pure, honest, lovely, just, and of a good report, you will be more conscious of God's Word than of your own personal feelings. It is much more important to walk in the peace of God than to carry "a chip on your shoulders."

Always remember that you can do all things *through Christ* who strengthens you (Philippians 4:13).

Love Doesn't Keep a List of Wrongs

Do not keep a list of wrongdoings, whether it be in a marriage relationship or in a friendship relationship. The God-kind of love *forgives* and *forgets* offenses. There is no recollection of wrongs.

Bringing up past grievances only heightens the wall between people, regardless of the type of relationship involved.

"When you forgive anyone, I do too...A further reason for forgiveness is to keep from being outsmarted by Satan; for we know what he is trying to do" (2 Corinthians 2:10,11, LIVING BIBLE).

Instant forgiveness will close the door to Satan and his schemes in your life. You cannot afford to keep a list of wrongs! Let go of them, and let God promote you to increased heights in Him!

Love Does Not Rejoice at Injustice, Is Not Happy When Evil Befalls Another, Does Not Rejoice Over Misfortunes of Others

When a person has been offended, he may initially think bad thoughts about the offender. God in His Word, however, gives us a directive for handling this type of situation.

"Follow peace with all men, and holiness, without which no man shall see the Lord: Looking diligently lest any man fail of the grace of God; lest any root of bitterness springing up trouble you, and thereby many be defiled" (Hebrews 12:14,15)

"If you love someone you will be loyal to him no matter what the cost. You will always believe in him, always expect the best of him, and always stand your ground in defending him" (1 Corinthians 13:7, LIVING BIBLE).

The Love of God Will Never Give Up on People

Jesus' love never gave up on the disciples, no matter how often they failed. John, the author of the three epistles on love, was the disciple Jesus called "the son of thunder," because he and his brother wanted to call fire down from heaven to consume the Samaritan village which did not receive them. Later John was to be called "the disciple of love." The Spirit of Christ transformed John's life, and it will also transform your life.

God's love never comes to an end. If you feel you are at the end of the rope in your faith for someone, don't give up. God's love will cause you to triumph in your stand. The love of God is the foundation for faith, for *"faith works by love"* (Galatians 5:6). God's love is our source of living.

Walking in love encompasses all of the fruit of the Spririt—and walking in love is walking in the Spirit!

Aids To Walking in Love

Some dynamic aids that will help you walk in love are:

1. Decide to love. Love is a decision, not a feeling.

2. Watch your mouth. *"Let no corrupt communication proceed out of your mouth, but that which is good to the use of edifying, that it may minister grace unto the hearers. And grieve not the holy Spirit of God, whereby ye are sealed unto the day of redemption. Let all bitterness, and wrath, and anger, and clamour, and evil speaking, be put away from you, with all malice: And be ye kind one to another, even as God for Christ's sake hath forgiven you"* (Ephesians 4:29-32).

3. Be the first to admit that you are wrong, and ask forgiveness no matter who is at fault.

4. Develop an openness with people. Endeavor to communicate in an honest, open way.

5. Pray in the Spirit. *"But you, beloved, build yourselves up [founded] on your most holy faith— make progress, rise like an edifice higher and higher—praying in the Holy Spirit; Guard and keep*

yourselves in the love of God; expect and patiently wait for the mercy of our Lord Jesus Christ, the Messiah, [which will bring you] unto life eternal" (Jude 20,21, AMPLIFIED).

6. Spend time **daily** in God's Word. *"But he who keeps [treasures] His Word—who bears in mind His precepts, who observes His message in its entirety—truly in him has the love of and for God been perfected (completed, reached maturity). By this we may perceive and know and recognize and be sure that we are in Him"* (1 John 2:5, AMPLIFIED).

7. Use your faith to believe that God's Word will be perfected in your life and in the lives of others.

3
Joy

The Kingdom of God does not consist of rules and regulations, do's and don'ts, but is a relationship of right standing with God resulting in peace and joy in the Holy Spirit. *"For the kingdom of God is not meat and drink; but righteousness, and peace, and joy in the Holy Ghost"* (Romans 14:17).

The greatest joy you can experience in this life is that of accepting Jesus Christ as your Lord and Savior. With this experience comes overwhelming joy, bubbling forth from deep within your heart.

Matthew 13:44 says, *"...the kingdom of heaven is like unto treasure hid in a field; the which when a man hath found, he hideth, and for joy thereof goeth and selleth all that he hath, and buyeth that field."* Second Corinthians 4:7 says that we have this treasure (Jesus) in our earthen vessel, and what a treasure He is!

Eternal Joy vs. Temporal Joy

There is a difference between eternal joy and temporal joy. Eternal joy is the product of Christ in you, while temporal joy is the product of natural circumstances. Second Corinthains 4:18 says, *"Since we consider and look not to the things that are seen but to the things that are unseen; for the things that are visible are temporal (brief and fleeting), but the things that are invisible are deathless and everlasting"* (AMPLIFIED). Another version says the things unseen are eternal.

Something temporary is subject to change in an instant, while something eternal will never change! Although Satan has a counterfeit for nearly everything God has, his goods are only temporary. Temporal joy may flee in a moment. Eternal joy—God's joy—remains forever!

Ecclesiastes 7:6 says, *"For as the crackling of thorn bushes under a pot, so is the laughter of the fool, and this too is futility."* (NAS BIBLE). Thorn bushes were used as fuel for fire because they burned up so quickly. Temporal joy is like these thorn bushes. It goes as quick as it comes.

My husband has told me about the excitement and joy he felt as a little boy during the Christmas holidays — the glitter of tinsel and the opening of gifts. But he said that when the holidays came to a close, he felt such emptiness, such a let down. What an accurate description of temporal joy! Temporal joy never quite measures up to your expectations.

Proverbs 14:13 says, *"Laughter cannot mask a heavy heart. When laughter ends, the grief remains"* (LIVING BIBLE). Many people in the world (and sometimes even Christians) have tried to cover deep wounds and hurts with a false mask of joy, but it is not difficult to distinguish genuine joy from counterfeit joy.

Eternal joy is not a frivolous joy; it is an inner joy, a knowing that God will never fail you, never leave you, nor will His Word return void in your life!

Joy Will Cause You To Stagger Not at God's Promises

Joy will help you keep a positive attitude and a smile on your face even while you are looking not at the things which are seen, but at the things which are not seen.

With the God-kind of joy, you are free to keep looking to the eternal Word, knowing and expecting God's Word to come alive in your life. You must be like Abraham, *"Who against hope believed in hope, that he might become the father of many nations, according to that which was spoken...He staggered not at the promise of God through unbelief; but was strong in faith, giving glory to God; And being fully persuaded that, what he had promised, he was able also to perform* (Romans 4:18,20,21).

In the midst of Abraham's circumstances, he glorified God. Acts 16 says that this is also what Paul and Silas did in the Philippian jail, when at midnight they worshipped and praised the Lord. An earthquake shook the prison doors open, and all of their bands were loosed.

Don't be mistaken: Paul and Silas were not rejoicing about their being in jail; they were rejoicing in spite of their circumstances.

In everything you are to give thanks, but not *for* everything. First Thessalonians 5:18 says, *"In every thing give thanks...."* Remember also that it is the devil who comes to steal, kill and destroy, while it is Jesus Christ who came to bring abundant life (John 10:10). Don't thank God for sickness, accidents, and untimely deaths. But thank God that He is still the Lord of lords and King of kings and His mercy endures forever.

When you are facing difficult circumstances, rejoice and thank the Lord that He is your Deliverer. You can rejoice in trying times because of who resides within you— Christ Jesus! In releasing the joy of the Lord in the midst of any circumstance, the bands of wickedness are loosed.

Praise and rejoicing drew the attention of unbelievers. Acts 16:25 says that the prisoners heard Paul and Silas rejoicing. They were awe struck at what they heard. When the prison doors opened supernaturally and the bands upon Paul and Silas fell off, the unbelievers were not even able to move. They were struck dumb momentarily by the power of God!

Praising the Lord will bring immediate results, some of which include:

1. Praise gets your mind off of you and onto the Lord.

2. Praise will shake the circumstances.

3. Praising and rejoicing in the Lord will open prison doors which have been locked in your life.

4. Praising and rejoicing in the Lord will loosen the bands of the devil from you and from those around you.

5. Praise brings the supernatural manifestations of God upon the scene, which may lead sinners to salvation.

Joy Brings Strength

Nehemiah 8:10 says, *"...the joy of the Lord is your strength."* If you let go of your joy, you let go of your strength. No man can take your joy from you. Neither can the devil take your joy from you. However, the devil will attempt to put so much pressure upon you that **you** will let go of your joy.

God's Word says, *"...be strong in the Lord, and in the power of his might"* (Ephesians 6:10).

Be joyful in the Lord, for then all weakness will leave you, and God's strength will sustain you in the midst of any situation.

Joy Brings Healing

"A happy heart is a good medicine and a cheerful mind works healing, but a broken spirit dries the bones" (Proverbs 17:22, AMPLIFIED).

Rejoicing in the Lord will actually loose the healing power of Jesus Christ to flow through your physical body. Medical science even has records of people with terminal illnesses who rejoiced their way back to health! We have a reason to rejoice because of what Jesus has done and will do for us.

Joy Works Patience

"Rejoice in the Lord always—delight, gladden yourselves in Him; again I say, Rejoice!" (Philippians 4:4, AMPLIFIED).

The joy that comes in praise and thanksgiving unto the Lord will work patience, strengthening your faith in the midst of trials. *"But let endurance and steadfastness and patience have full play and do a thorough work, so that you may be [people] perfectly and fully developed (with no defects), lacking in nothing"* (James 1:4, AMPLIFIED).

Joy in Doing God's Will

There is a joy in doing God's will. Psalm 40:8 says, *"I **delight** to do Your will, O my God"* (AMPLIFIED).

Jesus delighted in doing His Father's will. You are to delight in doing the Father's will also. God will reveal His plan and will for you if you seek Him with a pure heart. You will experience great joy in obedience as you follow God's plan for you! When we resist God's will, our joy leaves. Desire God's will for your life.

God's Word Illuminates Joy

Joy will come to you as you meditate upon God's Word. *"Your words were found, and I ate them, and Your word was to me a joy and the rejoicing of my heart..."* (Jeremiah 15:16, AMPLIFIED).

"Eating" God's Word is much like eating food. You must chew your food before it can be swallowed and digested! Many times truths from God's Word must be meditated upon before they become illuminated to your heart.

In my own life, certain Scriptures which I had previously memorized suddenly became alive in my spirit as I again meditated upon them and sang them to myself.

You will experience an overwhelming joy as the Word of God is illuminated in your heart and mind.

Joy Serves As a Protective Guard Against the Enemy

"Awake, awake; **put on your strength** (joy), *O Zion* (the church and you as an individual); ***put on your beautiful garments*** (praise), *O Jerusalem, the holy city; for henceforth there shall no more come into you the uncircumcised and the unclean* (sinful). ***Shake yourself*** *from the dust; arise, sit* [erect in a dignified place], *O Jerusalem;* **loose yourself from the bonds of your neck,** *O captive daughter of Zion"* (Isaiah 52:1,2, AMPLIFIED).

Dress yourself in the spiritual clothes of joy and praise. When you begin to rejoice in the Lord, you will actually feel yourself being liberated from things that have held you back—bonds of defeat, fear, inferiority, or weakness.

Jehoshaphat and the children of Israel sang and rejoiced their way to deliverance from the hand of their enemies in 2 Chronicles 20. As they sang praises, the Lord caused their enemies to destroy themselves.

Begin to praise the Lord and rejoice over Him and He will place a supernatural hedge about you to protect you from the darts, wiles, and schemes of the enemy. You will quickly see the devil confused and defeated and your circumstances changed in the presence of God's joy.

Joy Brings the Manifested Presence of Christ Upon the Scene

You may not always feel like rejoicing before the Lord. Your rejoicing may sometimes be offered as a sacrifice. A sacrifice is an offering you give that takes much effort because you don't feel like doing it. God says, "Give what you have, and I'll give you more." When you begin to rejoice in the Lord and praise Him, you actually will bring forth His manifested presence, and in His presence *"is fullness of joy"* (Psalm 16:11, AMPLIFIED).

"And now shall my head be lifted up above my enemies round about me; in His tent I will offer sacrifices and shouting of joy; I will sing, yea, I will sing praises to the Lord" (Psalm 27:6, AMPLIFIED).

Make a quality decision to daily offer adoration, love, prayer, and worship unto the Lord. It will pay rich dividends!

Avoid Blockages to Joy

Walking in the love of God and in the presence of God will bring fullness of joy into your life. Never allow unforgiveness, resentment, bitterness, or ill will to abide in your heart, for they will stop the flow of the joy of the Lord in your life. Other sins also will stop the flow of joy in your life.

When the Psalmist David realized that sin had robbed him of his joy in the Lord, he prayed, *"Create in me a clean heart, O God; and renew a right spirit within me...Restore unto me the joy of thy salvation..."* (Psalm 51:10,12). A clean heart and a renewed right spirit returned to David the joy of his salvation. When we keep our hearts clean before the Lord, God's joy can overflow into our lives.

Scriptural Ways To Release Joy and Praise to God

Scriptural ways to release joy and praise to the Lord include:

1. **With a song** - *"The Lord is my strength and my [impenetrable] shield; my heart trusts, relies on and confidently leans on Him, and I am helped; therefore my heart greatly rejoices, and with my song will I praise Him"* (Psalm 28:7, AMPLIFIED).

2. **With a shout** - *"But let all those who take refuge and put their trust in You rejoice; let them ever sing and shout for joy, because You make a covering over them and defend them; let those also who love Your name be joyful in You and be in high spirits"* (Psalm 5:11, AMPLIFIED).

3. **With musical instruments and with the dance** - *"Let them praise His name in chorus and choir and with the [single or group] dance, let them sing praises to Him with the tambourine and lyre!"* (Psalm 149:3, AMPLIFIED). *"Praise Him with tambourine and [single or group] dance; praise Him with stringed and wind instruments or flutes!"* (Psalm 150:4, AMPLIFIED).

4. **With the clapping of hands** - *"O clap your hands, all you peoples! Shout to God with the voice of triumph and songs of joy!"* (Psalm 47:1, AMPLIFIED).

5. **With uplifted hands** - *"So will I bless You while I live; I will lift up my hands in Your name"* (Psalm 63:4, AMPLIFIED).

4
Peace

God's promises of peace in the Word belong to you as a child of God. Believe them and receive them!

Isaiah 32:17 and 18 says, *"And* **the effect of righteousness shall be peace** *[internal and external], and the result of righteousness, quietness and confident trust for ever. My people shall dwell in a peaceable habitation, in safe dwellings, and in quiet resting places"* (AMPLIFIED).

Romans 5:1 says, "Therefore, **since we are justified**—*acquitted, declared righteous, and given a right standing with God—through faith let us [grasp the fact that we] have [the peace of reconciliation]* **to hold and to enjoy, peace with God through our Lord Jesus Christ,** *the Messiah, the Anointed One"* (AMPLIFIED).

The opposite of peace is fear, conflict, violence, or disorder. The peace of God brings freedom from strife—both internal and external. Strife can be all around you, but you won't experience discord if you remain in God's peace.

Jesus—The Greatest Example of Peace

Jesus is your greatest example of total peace. In the account of Mark 4, Jesus was asleep in the boat with His disciples when the winds and waves began to swell to hurricane proportions. The disciples became fearful. They forgot that the Creator of the universe, the Son of Almighty God, the "all-sufficient One," was in the boat with them!

The disciples awoke Jesus and said to Him. *"...Master, do You not care that we are perishing?"* (Mark 4:38, AMPLIFIED). In other words, "You should be worrying with us and at least lending a hand to bail the water out." They were not thinking that He could stop the storm.

Christians often react in the same way. We sometimes lose sight of the fact that the Son of God, the Son of the Highest, resides within us through the Holy Spirit. Many times we have prayed without really releasing any faith in God that He could change things — we have just prayed as a religious habit, still worrying after we prayed.

Jesus arose and rebuked the wind saying, "Peace, be still." He then turned to the disciples and asked, "Why are you so fearful? How is it that you have no faith?" In the stormy situations of your life, turn toward Jesus, for He will *never* leave you nor forsake you! He is always present with you. Through Him you can use the authority He has invested in you and speak to the situations you face, saying, "PEACE, BE STILL." Then cast the care on Him, and let Him carry it while you rest in His peace!

Heart Peace and Fear Don't Mix

I am frequently reminded of the memorable quote, "Fear knocked at the door. Faith answered, but no one was there!" Faith cannot operate when fear is present. Peace cannot flourish when fear is present either.

Where there is faith, there will be peace, even in the midst of the storms of life. Isaiah 26:3 says, *"You will guard him and keep him in perfect and constant peace whose mind [both its inclination and its character] is stayed on You, because he commits himself to You, leans on You and hopes confidently in You"* (AMPLIFIED). Peace will prevail when you keep your mind upon the Word of God. Peace will prevail when you speak the Word of God over situations that exist in your life—and watch the situations move while you remain stable (standing still)!

Philippians 4:7 says, *"And God's peace [be yours, that tranquil state of a soul assured of its salvation through Christ, and so fearing nothing from God and content with its earthly lot of whatever sort that is, that peace] which transcends all understanding, shall garrison and mount guard over your hearts and minds in Christ Jesus"* (AM-PLIFIED). When God's peace mounts guard over your heart and mind, none of the fiery darts of the enemy will be able to touch you. They may still try to come toward you, but the peace of God within you will repel them!

Jesus is speaking to you and me in John 14:27 when He says, *"Peace I leave with you; My [own] peace I now give and bequeath to you. Not as the world gives do I give to you. Do not let your heart be troubled, neither let it be afraid—stop allowing yourselves to be agitated and disturbed; and do not permit yourselves to be fearful and intimidated and cowardly and unsettled"* (AMPLIFIED).

Jesus is saying, "DON'T ALLOW THE HEART PEACE WHICH I HAVE FREELY GIVEN YOU AS MY CHILD TO BE RUFFLED, DISTURBED, OR

HINDERED IN ANY WAY. BUT LET THE HEART
PEACE WHICH I HAVE PLACED WITHIN YOU AND
ABOUT YOU DOMINATE YOU IN ALL SITUA-
TIONS!" In other words, the responsibility for staying in
peace, for letting peace dominate, and for letting God's
peace continue to grow, falls upon you and me!

God's Peace and the World's Peace Differ

God's peace is eternal, while the world's peace is only momentary. That is why, if we are anchored into Christ
Jesus and the Word of God, we cannot allow ourselves to
remain troubled or afraid when trouble comes.

The world is filled with instability and troubles in the
form of wars, unemployment, crimes, famines, bizarre
weather conditions, and turmoil, but Jesus is saying to you
and me today, *"I have told you these things so that in Me
you may have perfect peace and confidence. In the world
you have tribulation and trials and distress and frustra-
tion; but be of good cheer—take courage, be confident,
certain, undaunted—for **I have overcome the world—I
have deprived it of power to harm, have conquered it
[for you]"*** (John 16:33, AMPLIFIED).

The peace of God is beautifully displayed in the life
of Daniel, even though the world about him was everything
but peaceful. Daniel was given preference in the Kingdom
of King Darius because he had an excellent spirit.

Many people were jealous of Daniel and conspired
against him, causing the king to decree that any person
who petitioned any god or man other than the king would

be thrown to the lions.

Daniel, however, continued to pray and seek his God. He was then brought before the king to be charged for not obeying this decree. To the king's displeasure, he had no choice but to honor the decree and throw Daniel into the lion's den.

The king spent a sleepless night, with no peace, being in great fear for his favored servant, Daniel. Great peace, however, was exhibited in Daniel, for he was fully confident that God's hand of deliverance would bring him forth.

In this situation, Daniel's peace was not established or maintained by comfortable surroundings. Quite the contrary! He was in an impossible situation from the natural point of view!

The king was the one who experienced great turmoil, even though he was in the comfortable surroundings. You see, peace is not a *place*, but a state of being. Don't ever allow your peace to hinge on anything but your relationship with God.

Jesus walked in a state of peace despite the great demands placed upon Him. The masses surrounded Him constantly. There were times, however when Jesus stepped aside from the masses of people into a solitary place to spend time in prayer, **maintaining His intimate relationship** with the Father.

I remember one time while I was in prayer, the Spirit of God spoke to my heart and said, "Come apart, Sharon, before you come apart." So I know there are times when you must step aside from the busy daily routines and go to a place of solitude to receive from the Lord. Such a time never will be wasted! Rather, in this precious time with Him, a new pace will be set for your life. More than that, new growth in the area of peace will take place within you, for God's peace will flood your soul. His peace will saturate you anew! Take this time apart. It is a "must" in the life of any Christian.

Let Peace Rule in Your Life

"Let the peace of God be the umpire in your life" (Rotherham's translation of Colossians 3:15). The Amplified Bible says it this way: *"And let the peace (soul harmony which comes) from Christ rule (act as umpire continually) in your hearts—deciding and settling with finality all questions that arise in your minds—[in that peaceful state] to which [as members of Christ's] one body you were also called [to live]. And be thankful—appreciate, giving praise to God always."* An umpire in a softball game makes all of the final decisions on the plays. In seeking direction from God, the peace of God will reign when you are on the right path. His peace will guide you in making final decisions. Isaiah 55:12 says, *"...you shall go out with joy, and be led forth with peace"* if you've allowed God's Word to be settled in your heart.

We must allow God's peace to lead and control our lives if we are to live spiritually prosperous and if sinners are to be attracted to His life within us.

Matthew says, *"Blessed—enjoying enviable happiness, spiritually prosperous [that is, with life-joy and satisfaction in God's favor and salvation, regardless of their outward conditions]—are the makers and maintainers of peace, for they shall be called the sons of God!"* (Matthew 5:9, AMPLIFIED).

Let the peace implanted within you rule and reign so you will not only be a maker of peace, but you will also be a maintainer of peace in your life and in the lives of others!

5
Longsuffering

Webster defines longsuffering as "long and patient endurance of an offense." Moffatt's translation says longsuffering is "being good tempered." Phillips' translation calls it "patience." One of God's characteristics is longsuffering.

In Exodus 34, God proclaimed to Moses that He was the Lord God, *"merciful and gracious, longsuffering, and abundant in goodness and truth."*

Examples of Longsuffering

The children of Israel are a perfect example of God's longsuffering toward mankind. Throughout the 40 years they spent in the wilderness, they constantly complained and failed multitudes of times in keeping their covenant with God. But each time they cried out to God and repented of their sin, God in His infinite love, mercy, and longsuffering delivered them.

Every Christian has complained, disobeyed, or failed God in some way at some time in his life. Yet God always will extend His loving forgiveness and forbearance to you when you repent and turn again to Him.

In the book of Jonah, God chose to extend His mercy and longsuffering to Nineveh. That's why He sent Jonah to warn of coming judgment if they didn't repent. Jonah despised the Lord's longsuffering and goodness to the people of Nineveh. He **wanted** them to be punished for their sins.

Romans 2:4 says that we are not to despise the goodness, forbearance, and longsuffering of God, knowing that the goodness of God leads men to repentance.

You may know people who have failed God and who are now living in sin. Don't shun them, but pray for them. They are in need of God's love and mercy. God hasn't given up on them, and neither should we! God's longsuffering never gives up on people!

"The Lord is not slack concerning his promise, as some men count slackness; but is longsuffering to usward, not willing that any should perish, but that all should come to repentance" (2 Peter 3:9).

Longsuffering Toward Others

As a child of God, you have been called to be a minister of reconciliation (2 Corinthians 5:18) Many people will cross your path who need to be reconciled to God. Compassion and patience are of utmost importance when ministering to people when bringing them to the Lord and when nurturing them on to maturity.

*"And the servant of the Lord must not strive; but be gentle unto all men, apt to teach, **patient**, in meekness instructing those who oppose themselves; if God peradventure will give them repentance to the acknowledging of the truth; and that they may recover themselves out of the snare of the devil, who are taken captive by him at his*

will" (2 Timothy 2:24-26).

First Corinthians 13:4 says that *"love suffers long."* If we walk in love, patience (longsuffering) will be a natural by-product. Paul tells us in Colossians 3:14 that love is the bond of perfectness which binds together the Body of Christ. Longsuffering is like a tough fiber which keeps this love bond from breaking under stress and strain. All relationships will at times experience stress and strain, but the fruit of longsuffering will keep the bond intact.

Longsuffering is essential to a healthy marriage relationship or to any relationship. I've heard of many marriages being dissolved on the grounds of what is called "incompatibility." That is definitely not God's plan for any marriage. We've all been incompatible at times, but if we will let the Spirit of Jesus rise up inside of us, we can learn to be compatible.

I have a very compatible relationship with my husband, but we've had to work at it. There have been times when stress and strain have come against us, but we have not allowed it to overtake us. Instead, we have *determined* in our hearts *always* to overcome and *always* to move into new realms of love in Christ and with each other. We have *determined* to allow the fruit of longsuffering to bind our relationship with cords of love that never will be broken. Determination coupled with God's strength can do a lot for a marriage.

Longsuffering in the Development of Your Own Faith

The fruit of longsuffering is needed in the trial of your own faith, for longsuffering (patience) is not developed merely by the trial itself. Rather, it is developed **in** the trial when you turn to the Word of God and to prayer. Some have thought that the trials and tribulations develop longsuffering; however, many people have gone through trials and have turned away from God instead of to God. **Trials and tribulations have not always developed patience! However, a steady diet of God's Word and prayer will develop patience in your life whether you're in a difficult time or not. Growth should be a daily process, not merely an experience only for difficult times.**

James 1:2-4 says, *"My brethren, count it all joy when ye fall into divers temptations; knowing this, that the trying of your faith worketh patience. But let patience have her perfect work, that ye may be perfect and entire, wanting nothing."* James is not saying to be joyful **because** you are tempted, tested, or tried. He is saying, however, that **in the midst of** temptations, tests, and trials, you should begin to rejoice in the Lord. Godly longsuffering does not mean that you simply resign yourself to a position or an attitude of "I must just endure." The God-kind of longsuffering is not merely an endurance; rather, it is standing and maintaining an attitude of joy and a vision of God's Word perfecting everything that concerns you. It is simply another opportunity for the Word of God to prevail in your life.

The difference between endurance and godly longsuffering is the fruit of joy. In Colossians 1:11, Paul prayed that we would be strengthened with all might according to his glorious power, unto all patience and longsuffering with *joyfulness.*

Some people have not exercised the joy of the Lord with their longsuffering, not even making an effort to put a smile on their face. Instead, they have displayed the "poor little 'ol me" attitude. This attitude is not indicative of the fruit of the Spirit and actually drives away friends. Godly longsuffering will not bring attention to self but will glorify God.

James says if we let patience have her complete work, we will be perfectly and fully developed (with no defects), lacking in nothing.

The Scripture says we've been surrounded by a great cloud of witnesses (those saints who have gone on before us), who have stood on God's Word (Hebrews 12:1). Hebrews 6:12 says, *"...be not slothful, but followers of them who through **faith** and **patience** inherit the promises."* Faith coupled with patience will bring the fulfillment of God's Word in your life.

"Do not, therefore, fling away your fearless confidence, for it carries a great and glorious compensation of reward. For you have need of steadfast patience and endurance, so that you may perform and fully accomplish the will of God, and thus receive and carry away [and enjoy to the full] what is promised" (Hebrews 10:35,36, AMPLIFIED).

To walk in the Spirit, the servant of the Lord must pursue patience (longsuffering) in every area of his life.

6
Gentleness

Two of the fruit of the Spirit which are commonly confused, yet are distinctly different, are gentleness and meekness. Gentleness is an action we display, while meekness is a state of humility.

Donald Gee, in *Fruit of the Spirit,* describes gentleness as "strength or power under perfect control." Jesus had great strength and power, but it always was under the control of the Holy Spirit.

Jesus' Example of Gentleness

We see this controlled strength and power exemplified in Jesus' gentleness toward the woman who was caught in adultery (John 8:1-11).

The Pharisees, attempting to catch Jesus in error of the law, asked Him whether she should be stoned. He ignored them for a time. Then He stood up, and with great composure said to them, *"He that is without sin among you, let him cast the first stone"* (John 8:7). They departed one by one. Only Jesus and the accused woman remained. Jesus asked her, *"Woman, where are your accusers? Hath no man condemned thee?"* (John 8:10). She answered, *"No...no man, Lord"* (Verse 11). Jesus responded in gentleness (with deep compassion from His heart), *"Neither do I condemn thee. Go, and sin no more"* (John 8:11).

Jesus never condoned sin, but He always ministered His love toward the people held in its bondage. Jesus said that He came not to condemn the world, but to save it (John 3:17).

The gentleness of Jesus was experienced by the woman caught in adultery. Jesus didn't come to condemn her but to set her free with His love and truth. Jesus admonished the woman tenderly to go and sin no more. This response won her heart! She had never known such gentleness from any man, for people had always been harsh with her and had taken advantage of her. I believe from that day forth she followed Jesus.

People who continually point their fingers at the sin of others would do well to study this Scripture if they really desire to be like Jesus.

The Fruit of Gentleness Must Blossom in Serving Others

Paul instructed people with humility and tenderness to hear the Word of the Lord (2 Corinthians 10:1). When I think of gentleness, I think of expressions of tenderness and compassion. As ministers of the Gospel, we must learn to deal with people compassionately and gently. The servant of the Lord must know how to gently share God's words of encouragement and instruction with all peoples, regardless of the circumstances these people are in.

You must never wound someone, but rather lift them out of their circumstances onto the Word of God! Gentleness and patience *always* will change people, while striving with people never will change them. The Word of God must be ministered with **grace,** which is able to build and establish babes in the faith.

"And the servant of the Lord must not be quarrelsome—fighting and contending. Instead he must be kindly to every one and mild-tempered—preserving the bond of peace; he must be a skilled and suitable teacher, patient and forbearing and willing to suffer wrong. He must correct his opponents with courtesy and gentleness, in the hope that God may grant that they will repent and come to know the Truth—that is, that they will perceive and recognize and become accurately acquainted with and acknowledge it, And that they may come to their senses [and] escape out of the snare of the devil, having been held captive by him, [henceforth] to do His [God's] will" (2 Timothy 2:24-26, AMPLIFIED).

We must have such a compassion for people, especially for babes in Christ. We must be willing not only to impart the Gospel of Jesus Christ, but we must be willing to pour our very lives into them.

"But we behaved gently when we were among you, like a devoted mother nursing and cherishing her own children. So, being thus tenderly and affectionately desirous of you, we continued to share with you not only God's good news (the Gospel) but also our own lives as well, for you had become so very dear to us" (1 Thessalonians 2:7,8, AMPLIFIED).

Don't judge someone on the basis of immaturity, but reach out and help and lift and edify in the Name of Jesus. For you see, when a toddler is learning to walk, he will fall down many times. His mother, however, won't scold him for falling. She will gently pick him up and set him on his feet to try again. She patiently and repeatedly reassures him until the toddler is able to walk without falling. Likewise, babes in Christ may take a few tumbles as they are learning to walk with God. However, those who are mature must be encouragers, gently lifting them with the Word and love of God.

"Behold, My Servant Whom I have chosen, My Beloved in and with Whom My soul is well pleased and has found its delight. I will put My Spirit upon Him, and He shall proclaim and show forth judgment to the nations. He will not strive or wrangle or cry out loudly, nor will any one hear His voice in the streets; A bruised reed He will not break, and a smoldering (dimly burning) wick He will not quench till He brings justice and a just cause to victory" (Matthew 12:18-20, AMPLIFIED). The bruised reed and the smoking flax represent weak young Christians who are not yet established in their faith. They may still have some traits that present difficulties in walking the Christian life. Jesus will not discourage, reject, or cast them away, but in gentle compassion, He will urge them on to maturity. And to express His gentle compassion, Jesus must have you and me through whom He can work! We are to be like Jesus in this world (1 John 4:17).

You will prove whether you are a minister of God or a minister of reconciliation by your expressions of kindness and gentleness with others. I am not saying that we should never be firm and straight-forward with people when they need it, but we can instruct them in a gentle way.

The dove has become a Christian symbol of simplicity, gentleness, and peace. A dove is known for his peaceful disposition, cleanness, and innocence. A dove will not retaliate against his enemies. I am not referring to the enemy—the devil—here, because we must retaliate or resist him, but we cannot win people by retaliating against them with natural means.

Jesus said that His children should be as wise as serpents and as harmless (gentle, guileless, and innocent) as doves (Matthew 10:16). In one sense, we are to be like the serpent, who never exposes himself to attack. The serpent is cautious, sharpsighted, discerning, and knowing. Jesus implied that His children are also to be cautious, sharpsighted, discerning, and knowing. At the same time, however, we must be like the dove, who remains at peace, in innocence, and cleanness from any sin. The children of God are to be guileless (honest and sincere with no deceit). God also has promised to be our shield and defender if we trust Him to be.

Jesus displayed wisdom in discerning the character of Judas Iscariot. He knew all the time that Judas would betray Him, yet Jesus was still gentle and compassionate toward Judas. It was this gentleness of Jesus which would not permit Him to retaliate against Judas. For *"...the wisdom that is from above is first pure, then peaceable, **gentle**..."* (James 3:17).

Judas Iscariot did not respond to the gentleness of Christ. Thus his life ended in disaster.

David the Psalmist, on the other hand, submitted to

the gentle workings of God in his life, which resulted in his success and exaltation. He wrote in Psalm 18:35, *"...thy gentleness hath made me great."* Had it not been for the gentleness of God, David would not have overcome the obstacles in his life and risen to greatness.

God's gentleness is much like the touch of a potter at his wheel. The sensitivity of His fingers can, with the slightest touch of the clay, bring permanent shape. God works gently in our lives, because He knows we are just like a piece of clay. Psalm 103:14 says, *"For he knoweth our frame; he remembereth that we are dust."* God is molding you and me into vessels of honor.

Our flesh often experiences the pressure of this inner working at the hand of God. First Peter 4:1 says, *"Forasmuch then as Christ hath suffered for us in the flesh, arm yourselves likewise with the same mind: for he that hath suffered in the flesh hath ceased from sin."* When you were born again, you were perfected on the inside (in your spirit), not on the outside. The flesh ceases from the sin as the Spirit of God prevails in your life.

Many newborn creatures in Christ Jesus still have habits and sins which God must gently remove from their lives by a work of the Holy Spirit. The Holy Spirit will gently change desires and habits, conforming the children of God to the image of Christ.

*"And so, as those who have been chosen of God, holy and beloved, put on a heart of compassion, kindness, humility, **gentleness** and patience"* (Colossians 3:12, NAS BIBLE).

7
Goodness

"In the beginning God created the heaven and the earth...and God saw every thing that He had made, and, behold, it was very good..." (Genesis 1:1,31). The beauty of a blazing sunset or the quiet serenity of a meadow after a spring rain confirm the greatness and goodness of God.

Psalm 33:5 says, *"...the earth is full of the goodness of the Lord."* God created the whole earth for the habitation and enjoyment of man. What a good Father to provide the best for His children! Oral Roberts, an evangelist and a minister of healing, has publicly proclaimed for years the fact that "God is a good God."

God's Highest Gift of Goodness To Man

God is *so good* that He gave His most precious and most valuable gift to man—the gift of His only begotten Son, JESUS. *"For God so greatly loved and dearly prized the world that He [even] gave up His only-begotten (unique) Son, so that whoever believes in (trusts, clings to, relies on) Him shall not perish—come to destruction, be lost—but have eternal (everlasting) life. For God did not send the Son into the world in order to judge—to reject, to condemn, to pass sentence on—the world; but that the world might find salvation and be made safe and sound through Him"* (John 3:16,17, AMPLIFIED).

People are drawn to God because of His goodness and mercy. His love for mankind is exhibited "in spite of," not "because of" what man has done or become. No one but our heavenly Father could love past man's faults and failures.

"Goodness" Is the Nature of the Father

Jesus is the expressed will of God. He said, *"If you have seen me, you have seen the Father"* (John 14:9). In viewing the life of Jesus, we can clearly see that God's will for us is good. Acts 10:38 says, *"How God anointed Jesus of Nazareth with the Holy Ghost and with power: who went about doing good, and healing all that were oppressed of the devil; for God was with him."* Jesus said, *"...I have come to give you life and give it more abundantly"* (John 10:10). It is the devil who comes to steal, to kill, and to destroy. Some people have been taught that God uses sickness and tragedy to discipline and teach His children. However, God has no sickness and tragedy. These are works of the devil to try to steal, kill, and destroy us. God is the good Father, who is always standing by willing to heal and to help us.

As a good Father, His instruments of correction are His rod (His Word) and His staff (His Spirit). The Psalmist David said, *"...thy rod and thy staff they comfort me"* (Psalm 23:4). The Father offers discipline in the highest form of love, for He said, *"All Scripture is given by inspiration of God, and is profitable...for **reproof**, for **correction**, and for **instruction** in righteousness"* (2 Timothy 3:16). Not only do we receive correction through the Word of God, but Jesus said, *"...the words that I speak unto you, they are spirit, and they are life"* (John 6:63). God's very words fill us with His life! And the abundance of God's life includes health, prosperity, joy, peace, and *all* the goodness of God.

People Known for the Fruit of Goodness

The fruit of goodness flowed through many of the followers of Christ, revealing this characteristic of their Father. In Acts 9, a woman named Dorcas, a disciple of Christ, who was a woman "full of good works," supervised a group of women who met the needs of many of the poor people of their day. Her untimely death brought much dismay to those who labored with her. She was considered so needful to the work of the kingdom that Peter raised her from the dead so she would be able to fulfill the ministry to which she had been called. Dorcas provoked others to love and to good works. I'm sure you can think of many brethren who provoke you unto love and good works. *"And let us consider one another to provoke unto love and to good works"* (Hebrews 10:24).

Joseph of Arimathea, noted as a just counselor and a "good" man, went to Pilate to ask for the body of Jesus. With great love and compassion, he took the body of his Lord from the cross to prepare for burial. His benevolence led him to give his own tomb for a place where Jesus could be laid.

Acts 11:24 says that Barnabas was *"a good man, full*

of the Holy Ghost and of faith." He gave his money to the poor and proved himself to be a hard worker among the people. Both the apostles and the common people recognized his goodness and trusted him.

Let the Fruit of Goodness Flourish in Your Life

Agathosune is the Greek word for "goodness" in the Scriptures. It means "the state of being good, kind, benevolent, generous, and God-like in life and conduct." When you are born again, you receive the fruit of goodness, but like the other fruit at this stage, it is only a seed and must be nourished with the Word of God to grow and produce in your life.

You no longer have to work with the idea of trying to be good; but instead, simply allow the nature of Christ to mature in you and then flow out from you!

You are not saved by your own good works, but by faith you receive Jesus into your heart. However, good works will accompany the salvation experience. *"For we are his workmanship, **created in Christ Jesus unto good works,** which God hath before ordained that we should walk in them"* (Ephesians 2:10). The good works actually are working out (carrying out) your salvation—becoming a doer of the Word that has been heard and received. *"Wherefore, my beloved, as ye have always obeyed, not as in my presence only, but now much more in my absence, **work out** (cultivate, carry out to the goal and fully complete) your own salvation with fear and trembling. For it is God which worketh in you both to will and to do of his* *good pleasure"* (Philippians 2:12,13).

Paul exhorts Christians to cultivate the fruit of their salvation. In Luke 6:43-45, Jesus says that a good tree brings forth good fruit, and a corrupt tree brings forth corrupt fruit. He goes on to say that every tree is known by its fruit. The good works which accompany your salvation are a reflection of the life of Christ within you.

Jesus redeemed you that you might be a peculiar people, zealous of good works. *"Who gave himself for us, that he might redeem us from all iniquity, and purify unto himself a peculiar people, zealous of good works"* (Titus 2:14). The Scriptures are full of examples of men and women who consecrated themselves unto the Lord for good works. The natural flow of the fruit of goodness was abundant in their lives.

Paul admonishes Christians always to follow that which is good. *"See that none render evil for evil unto any man; but ever follow that which is good, both among yourselves, and to all men"* (1 Thessalonians 5:15). Matthew 5:16 also says, *"Let your light so shine before men, that they may see your good works, and glorify your Father which is in heaven."* Your Christian lifestyle should so exhibit the character of Christ that all men will be drawn unto Him. Your light should be consistent in the words you speak and the life you live.

Paul prayed that the Church of Colosse *"...might walk worthy of the Lord unto all pleasing, being fruitful in every good work, and increasing in the knowlege of God"* (Colossians 1:10). You and I will benefit greatly by using his Scripture as a prayer today.

The fruit of goodness can be compared to natural mineral salt. The Scripture says that you and I are the salt of the earth and that salt is good. Salt is found everywhere—in animals, in vegetables, in minerals, in caves, and in the ocean. And so it is with God's children— they can be found everywhere! People are being saved in every walk in life, and the presence of these newly born-again people is as salt which acts as a preservative. The Christian's presence in the earth is the preserving factor to keep the forces of evil (decay) from bringing total destruction upon the earth.

Salt makes people thirsty. As a Christian, your presence should make people thirsty for God! When you are around a non-Christian and he sees how blessed you are and how effectively you are able to deal with life's problems, he will desire what you have. The peace you reflect, the joy of your countenance, and the overall lifestyle of goodness you possess will have a great impact on others.

If you are careful to behave honorably among unsaved people — even if they are suspicious of you or talk against you — they will end up praising God for your good works. *"Having your conversation honest among the Gentiles: that, whereas they speak against you as evildoers, they may by your good works, which they shall behold, glorify God in the day of visitation"* (1 Peter 2:12).

Salt is a healing agent. *You* are God's healing agent in the earth because of the Holy Spirit residing within you. You are able to speak words of healing to those around you. The Word of God within you has the power to set at liberty those who are bruised and deliver those who are held captive. Some people need an inner healing; others need physical healing. God has given His Word and His Spirit so you can minister to all kinds of people in all kinds of situations. God has no alternative but to use people—you and me—as channels of His love and power in this earth.

Just as salt will melt ice, God will use you and the warmth of your words to melt the coldness and hardness of people's hearts. The warm glow of the Holy Spirit in your life will draw them to Jesus!

Even though salt is good, if it has lost its flavor, what good is it? *"You are the salt of the earth, but if salt has lost its taste—its strength, its quality—how can its saltness be restored? It is not good for anything any longer but to be thrown out and trodden under foot by men"* (Matthew 5:13, AMPLIFIED). Salt which has lost its flavor is fit for nothing, not even for fertilizer. It is thrown out, and men trample it under foot. Some who have lost the fervor of God's Spirit have been trampled under foot by people in this world. But you, unlike the salt, can become full of flavor again if you turn and seek God. Do not allow slothfulness or the cares of this life rob you of your usefulness (of the salt in you). Instead, endeavor to remain a vessel of honor, sanctified and meet for the Master's use.

God's goodness is in you. His power is within you, helping you to live the Christian life. God shows us in Micah 6:8 how to walk in His goodness. *"He has showed you, O man, **what is good**; and what does the Lord require of you, but **to do justly**, and **to love kindness** and*

mercy, and to humble yourself and walk humbly with your God?" (AMPLIFIED).

And oh, what a comfort it is to know that God surrounds His children with goodness and mercy as we put our trust in Him. *"Surely goodness and mercy shall follow me all the days of my life..."* (Psalm 23:6).

8
Faithfulness

Just as there are several connotations for the word "love," you also will find three different meanings for the word "faith" as used in the New Testament. There is the **simple faith** by which you are saved. *"For by grace are ye saved through faith..."* (Ephesians 2:8). Then there is **the gift of faith**, which is given in order to meet special needs supernaturally (1 Corinthians 12:9). The faith that will be discussed in this chapter, however, is **the fruit of the Spirit**—faith (Galatians 5:22). I will refer to it as "faithfulness" rather than faith since this is the interpretation of this particular word in this Scripture.

Faithfulness can be defined as "trustworthiness, loyalty, reliability, constancy, steadfastness, and sincerity."

God's Example of Faithfulness

There is no greater example of faithfulness—trustworthiness, loyalty, reliability, constancy, steadfastness, and sincerity—than that of our Father God. *"It is of the Lord's mercies and loving-kindnesses that we are not consumed, because His (tender) compassions fail not. They are new every morning; great and abundant is your stability and* **faithfulness*** (Lamentations 3:22,23,AMPLIFIED).

God is and always has been faithful to keep His covenant with men. Even when men are not faithful, God remains faithful. God's faithfulness is revealed to us time and time again through His relationship with the children of Israel. Although the children of Israel rejected God many times, He always remained loyal to His covenant with them. Every time they called to Him, He displayed His faithfulness in power and greatness. He continually delivered them from their sin and their enemies. *"My covenant will I not break or profane, nor alter the thing that is gone out of My lips"* (Psalm 89:34, AMPLIFIED).

As born-again believers, we have a covenant with God through Jesus Christ our Mediator. This is a new and better covenant, because it is established on better promises (Hebrews 8:6). It is a covenant of grace. If we sin or fail to keep our part of the covenant, we have only to confess (repent of) our sins, for God's grace is ever ready to restore our fellowship with Him. *"If we [freely] admit that we have sinned and confess our sins, He is faithful and just [true to His own nature and promises] and will forgive our sins (dismiss our lawlessness) and continuously cleanse us from all unrigheousness—everything not in conformity to His will in purpose, thought and action"* (1 John 1:9, AMPLIFIED).

It is through the blood of Jesus that we are cleansed and reconciled back to God, for Hebrews 2:17 says that Jesus is a faithful, merciful High Priest for us. Jesus stands in the gap, always interceding to keep us reconciled to God.

Jesus' Example of Faithfulness

If you look at the faithfulness of Jesus to His Father, you will see that faithfulness sometimes must go beyond your own feelings. *"Wherefore in all things it behoved him to be made like unto his brethren, that he might be a merciful and **faithful** high priest in things pertaining to God, to make reconciliation for the sins of the people. For in that he himself hath suffered being tempted, he is able to succour them that are tempted. Wherefore, holy brethren, partakers of the heavenly calling, consider the Apostle and High Priest of our profession, Christ Jesus; who was **faithful** to him that appointed him..."* (Hebrews 2:17,18, and 3:1,2).

Jesus had to remain faithful to His Father's will by going through the cross experience, suffering the agony of it to provide salvation for us. He died and was resurrected that we might be made the righteousness of God in Christ (2 Corinthians 5:21). The Scripture says in Hebrews 12 that Jesus endured the cross for the joy that was set before Him. Jesus had to press beyond His momentary feeling to a greater joy of reward. He could rejoice, knowing that many would come into the Kingdom because of His obedience.

Let the Fruit of Faithfulness Mature in You

There are times when God will prove your faithfulness. He often will place you in seemingly unimportant positions, all the while watching to observe your faithfulness in the little things. God never will promote a person who is not faithful (responsible) in the little things.

The Scripture says in Nehemiah 13:13 that there were found four men in Israel who were counted faithful. They were placed as treasurers over the storerooms in the house of God to distribute grain, wine, and oil to their brethren. Their faithfulness was observed before they were given this task. The quicker you and I learn this lesson, the quicker God will use us in the work of His Kingdom!

In looking at the parable of the talents, the Master said in Matthew 25:21, *"...Well done, you upright (honorable, admirable) and faithful servant! You have been faithful and trustworthy over a little; I will put you in charge of much. Enter into and share the joy—the delight, the blessedness— which your master [enjoys]"* (AMPLIFIED).

A faithful servant always will be trusted to handle his responsibilities wisely, to the best of his ability. A faithful servant always is dependable. When given a task, he will complete it. He deals honestly in the affairs of life. When he sees something that needs to be done, he is willing to go beyond what is expected of him to do it. And finally, the person who is faithful is the one who enters into the joy of the Lord.

The reward of the good and faithful servant was added responsibility as well as the privilege of entering into the joy of the Lord. There always is overwhelming joy which comes with obedience. God can promote you when you are faithful. *"I give thanks to Him Who has granted me (the needed) strength and made me able [for this], Christ Jesus our Lord, because He has judged and counted me faithful and trustworthy, appointing me to [this steward-ship of] the ministry"* (1 Timothy 1:12, AMPLIFIED). To you who desire a greater ministry, God is saying, "BE FAITHFUL WHERE YOU ARE, AND I WILL ADVANCE YOU IN DUE TIME."

"So then let us [apostles] be looked upon as ministering servants of Christ and stewards (trustees) of the mysteries—that is, the secret purposes—of God. Moreover, it is [essentially] required of stewards that a man should be found faithful—proving himself worthy of trust" (1 Corinthians 4:1,2, AMPLIFIED).

One of the servants in Matthew 25 was found unfaithful. Three characteristics of an unfaithful servant, typical of some of God's servants today, are brought out in Dakes Reference Bible.

1. He accused his Master in order to excuse his own slothfulness. His accusation was not true, however. If the Master had indeed reaped where He had not sown, He would not have been a man of great wealth. The servant's attempt to shift the blame to his Master merely reveals his own attitude of laziness and insecurity.

2. The slothful person thinks that everything other people do prospers. He, however, is always failure-conscious. He usually thinks other people just hit lucky streaks. Don't let the enemy trick you with this kind of thinking! Joshua 1:8 tells us what a man must do if he expects to prosper: *"This book of the law shall not depart out of your mouth, but you shall meditate on it day and night, that you may observe and do according to all that is written in it; for then you shall make your way prosperous, and then you shall deal wisely and have good success"* (AMPLIFIED).

3. A slothful person always is afraid to venture out in business or take risks. He is afraid to step out in faith. However, a faithful person will step out as God reveals

things to him, knowing that God will always (without fail) bring to pass those things He has made known to him. Sometimes God might expect you to step out farther than you can clearly see, but He will always uphold you.

The Spirit of God always will encourage you to take ever-bigger steps of faith. That's the way to let the fruit of faithfulness (as well as all of the other fruit) mature in you.

Many people have tremendous potential, but they have not been faithful. Sometimes a faithful person who isn't necessarily the most talented will be promoted over a highly talented person simply because of faithfulness. It's the same way within a ministry. People sometimes wonder why they haven't been promoted into advanced positions as quickly as others, but my first question would be "Have they been faithful? Have they fulfilled the tasks they have been given, even though they may seem like small tasks?"

Proverbs 25:19 refers to an unfaithful servant. *"Confidence in an unfaithful man in time of trouble is like a broken tooth, and a foot out of joint."* An unfaithful person is like a pain or a problem, while a faithful person is like a good tooth, never offering a pain or a problem, but **always dependable.** Don't be like the unfaithful servant!

God is well able to take an unfaithful person and transform him into a faithful person through the power of the Holy Spirit. For example, even though Peter denied Jesus three times, it was evident he had become a different man by the Day of Pentecost. He had become faithful to

God, faithful to what God had called him to do, and faithful to proclaim with boldness God's Word everywhere he went. The power of the Holy Spirit definitely can produce faithfulness in a person who has previously had no capacity for it.

God is calling His people to commitment and to faithfulness. In the past few years, some people within the Body of Christ have hopped from one church to another, "skimming the cream off the milk," so to speak. There is nothing wrong with visiting different churches occasionally, but God wants to get His people past the "floating around" stage into a stable commitment to one church body so they can grow and mature to their maximum potential. (And God's potential for His committed children is unlimited!) We must grow beyond the "I don't want to get tied down" syndrome.

In committing to one church body, it is like drinking whole milk. A steady diet of cream will not allow for proper growth. God has provided for your overall development through the establishment of the local church, but commitment requiring involvement and faithfulness is essential. Sometimes your faithfulness to a local church body will determine the effectiveness of the entire Body of Christ. My dad used to say, "If everyone in this church was just like me, what kind of a church would this church be?"

Are you faithful in your attendance, your tithes, your abilities, your prayers, and in the time given to the work of the Lord? What an impact the church would have on a community — and even the world — if all its members were found faithful!

Rewards of Faithfulness

There will be times when commitment and faithfulness will require you to push beyond your own personal desires. For example, the role of a mother involves this type of commitment. She is fully committed to meet her child's every need. Even when there are other things she might prefer to do, her commitment to the child comes first. Proverbs 31:28 says the reward of a faithful mother is that *"her children will rise up and call her blessed...."*

There are rewards for the faithful servant, too!

1. *"A faithful man shall abound with blessings..."* (Proverbs 28:20)

2. *"O love the Lord, all ye his saints: for the Lord preserveth the faithful"* (Psalm 31:23).

3. *"...thou hast been faithful over a few things, I will make thee ruler over many things..."* (Matthew 25:21).

4. *"...he counted me faithful, putting me into the ministry"* (1 Timothy 1:12).

5. *"...be thou faithful unto death, and I will give thee a crown of life"* (Revelation 2:10).

9
Meekness

Meekness may be defined as "mildness, forbearance, or a state of being submissive and humble." Probably the best definition of meekness is "total dependence upon God."

Some translations interchange gentleness and meekness. Gentleness is something you say or do, while meekness is a state of being. Unbelievers sometimes are able to express gentleness, but because of their unregenerate hearts, they eventually revert back to pride and anger. Meekness is displayed when a person is able to control his mind, will, and emotions (his soulish realm). He has trained his soulish realm to submit to the Spirit of God. He does not tolerate thoughts of anger, pride, jealousy, or competition to be a part of his new nature in Christ Jesus.

You must realize that meekness is **not** weakness. Quite the contrary! It takes great strength of character to be a meek person.

Moses: An Example of Excellence in the Fruit of Meekness

Let's take a look at Moses, the man the Bible calls the meekest person on the face of the earth (Numbers 12:3). Moses had been brought up in Pharaoh's household and received the best in education and training. When he realized the call God had placed upon him to free His people, Israel, from the Egyptian oppression, Moses tried to deliver them in his own ability. He knew the "will" of God, but he needed further instructions, as he did not have the "how" or the "when" to fulfill God's plan.

Some have missed God's highest plan because they have stopped short. They have failed to get full details for God's special plans. And this is comparable to baking a cake. You not only need the recipe's required ingredients, but you also must read the directions for "fulfillment" of the project—excellence in eating!

After Moses failed to free the people because he relied on his own strength, he fled into the wilderness, but he could not escape the call of God. No one is truly able to escape the call of God that is upon his or her life. Moses, while in the wilderness, came into the presence of God, and in this inimate fellowship with His Father, he was able to face the total failure of his own ability: his sufficiency was not in himself, but in God.

Second Corinthians 3:5 and 6 says, *"Not that we are fit (qualified and sufficient in ability) of ourselves to form personal judgments or to claim or count anything as coming from us; but our power and ability and sufficiency are from God. [It is He] Who has qualified us (making us to be fit and worthy and sufficient) as ministers and dispensers of a new covenant [of salvation through Christ], not [ministers] of the letter—that is, of legally written code— but of the Spirit; for the code [of the law] kills, but the (Holy) Spirit makes alive."* (AMPLIFIED).

God will not throw away your talents, education, or training, but He will bring you to a place of **total dependence upon Him** rather than letting you depend upon your own abilities.

Too many times people lean upon their own abilities. This binds the hand of God (limits Him), preventing Him from using them in a mighty way. Because Moses leaned entirely upon God, the Father God, Jehovah, was able to use the training Moses had received in Pharaoh's house. You will notice that Moses kept an attitude of meekness even after becoming a successful leader. This was because he was totally dependent upon and submitted to God.

Many people don't want to submit to others because they are not submitted to "THE AUTHORITY"—God's authority. We first must be submitted to God. Submission is a word which has been widely misunderstood. It actually means "yielded obedience." It should be our highest desire and constant goal to obey the moment God speaks.

You often can learn spiritual lessons such as submission from the natural realm, either at home or at your place of employment. Learn to submit to those in authority over you. Children who are raised to submit to their parents will be more quick to submit to an employer on a job. It will also be easier to submit to God as they grow into adulthood. This principle works in another way, too. When a person strives to submit to God, he will be more submissive to earthly authorities. God cannot use you extensively until you learn to be submissive to His commands and His will.

Moses faced not only physical obstacles (such as the Red Sea), but he had to deal with constant murmuring and complaining from his people. Moses' own brother and sister, Aaron and Miriam, his closest companions, began to speak against him, even questioning his authority as a leader. Moses retained a meek attitude before his accusers, **bringing no defense in his own behalf.** Maturity in the fruit of meekness will cause the development of forbearance in dealing with people.

The Scripture says the Lord Himself spoke from heaven commanding Moses, Miriam, and Aaron to come into the tabernacle. God then appeared in a pillar of cloud, and His anger was kindled against Miriam and Aaron. Miriam was immediately struck with leprosy, while Aaron repented and pleaded in Miriam's behalf. Moses also interceded for God to heal Miriam. God required Miriam to remain outside the camp for seven days before she became totally clean—time enough to think about what she had done in speaking against God's anointed. I would imagine that she never again spoke against Moses!

The Word of God says, *"...Touch not mine anointed, and do my prophets no harm"* (1 Chronicles 16:22). Be cautious about speaking against brothers and sisters in Christ and against God's ministers, no matter what you think is wrong or what you see wrong. Instead of criticizing, murmuring, and complaining, immediately go to prayer in their behalf. Prayer still changes things today! Prayer will change you, and it also will change people and circumstances.

Time and time again, Moses interceded for the people, even though they still murmured against him. It takes great strength of character and tremendous forbearance to do that.

Along with the privilege of being a leader, Moses shouldered the massive responsibility of an entire nation — for with the privileges of leadership come great responsiblities.

Let Meekness Flourish in You

If you ever are placed in a position of leadership, there may be times when you will have to be forbearing with others, regardless of their actions toward you. If a leader does not walk in the spirit of meekness and forbearance, he eventually may find himself relieved of his position of leadership and authority.

Jesus was forbearing with His disciples and with the masses of people who thronged Him. A graphic illustration of His forbearance is seen in the situation where several mothers brought their children to Him to receive His blessing. The disciples considered this a waste of Jesus' precious time and openly attempted to discourage the mothers, but Jesus overheard the disciples and summoned the mothers to bring their children to Him. He patiently explained to the disciples that it is often the small things in life which are the most important. Such patient forbearance always will be exhibited by a good leader.

You can learn more about meekness through Jesus' example. Jesus said, *"Come unto me, all ye that labour and are heavy laden, and I will give you rest. Take my yoke upon you, and* **learn of me; for I am meek and lowly in heart;** *and ye shall find rest unto your souls"* (Matthew 11:28,29).

The opposite of meekness is pride. In John 3:30, John the Baptist said, *"He must increase, and I must decrease."* John realized that if God's Kingdom was to come and His will be done, he must be selfless and filled with God. The big "I" must die! The big "I" has to do with pride. Proverbs 16:18 says, *"Pride goest before destruction...."* A successful minister must be wary of this subtle tactic of the devil. **God wants you to be successful, but He doesn't want success to have you!**

"But this is not to be so among you; instead, whoever desires to be great among you must be your servant, And whoever wishes to be most important and first in rank among you must be the slave of all. For even the Son of man came not to have service rendered to Him, but to serve, and to give His life a ransom for (instead of) many" (Mark 10:43-45, AMPLIFIED). In keeping this Scripture, you will keep yourself from pride and destruction.

God's Commandments Regarding Meekness

God gives His children many commandments (not options) in His Word concerning meekness:

1. Galatians 6:1 says, *"Brethren, if a man be overtaken in a fault, ye which are spiritual, restore such an one in the spirit of meekness; considering thyself, lest thou also be tempted."* In this Scripture, Paul was speaking to mature Christians. He knew that the immature Christian would

have a tendency to be judgmental and critical rather than encouraging, exhorting, upholding, and uplifting of the one who had fallen.

The spiritually mature person will not need to know all the "juicy" details of a situation to minister and pray for the person's restoration. The mature Christian will seek to restore this person in love. Second Timothy 2:25 and 26 says, *"He must correct his opponents with courtesy and gentleness, in the hope that God may grant that they will repent and come to know the Truth—that is, that they will perceive and recognize and become accurately acquainted with and acknowledge it, And that they may come to their senses [and] escape out of the snare of the devil, having been held captive by him, [henceforth] to do His [God's] will"* (AMPLIFIED).

When you and I minister to those who are going through difficult times, we must be saturated with the meekness, humility, and love of our Father God, realizing that we ourselves are still human and have made mistakes. But, thank God, He never leaves us in our failures but brings us out to victory when we turn to Him.

2. First Peter 3:15 says, *"...be ready always to give an answer to every man that asketh you a reason of the hope that is in you with meekness and fear."* If someone questions you concerning your joy (and people will when the life of Christ Jesus is reflected through you), respond to them in meekness, and share with them the joy of your salvation. Some people in the world have been "turned off" because of some Christians displaying a self-righteous attitude and condemning them rather than loving them in-

to the Kingdom of God. People will receive more readily from someone who is not looking down on them.

I remember one time when my husband and I were traveling with our two babies, and we had to wait in the Chicago Airport eight hours for our flight. Because of a strike, many flights had been cancelled. As we waited, my little two-year-old daughter began to sing some Scripture songs while she played with her coloring books and doll. I made a determined effort to let God's joy and peace dominate me while we waited, for I knew my children would then be peaceful too. After a while, a lady sitting across from us came over to talk with us. She began complimenting my little girl's behavior, and I began to tell her about how the Lord had changed our lives. After she listened for a while, she asked me where we were from. I told her we were from Tulsa, Oklahoma.

She said, "You must know of Oral Roberts." "Yes," I replied, "We have been students at Oral Roberts University." She then shared that through Brother Roberts' ministry her husband had been totally delivered from alcohol and healed. I told her that Jesus wanted to come into her heart. We prayed together (she prayed the sinner's prayer), and she received Jesus into her heart. She was so elated after we prayed that she couldn't stop smiling or thanking me. I then shared with her how she could keep the joy and assurance of her salvation.

She told me, "I said to myself, 'That girl sitting across from me is going to bring **something good** into my life.'"

"Jesus is that something you were wanting," I assured her.

We left each other in an atmosphere of total joy, knowing God had planned our meeting that day. You see, she had been drawn to me and my children by the peace and joy of the Lord which she saw in our lives. Then, as I shared with her in the spirit of meekness, she was willing to receive.

3. James 1:21 says for us to receive the engrafted word with **meekness.** God taught me a lesson on meekness while my husband and I were attending Bible School. We had been in Tulsa prior to attending this school, and we had heard many great teachers of God's Word. Another couple who sat close to us had come to the summer session from California. The speaker for the week was a man we had heard before, and his teaching was on a subject we were already familiar with. While the other couple was elated over the teaching, I was sitting there with a "know-it-all" attitude, thinking to myself, *It's wonderful for all these people to hear this, but I've heard it before and could teach it myself!*

By the second class session, God spoke to me, telling me to keep a meek attitude for then, even though I had heard these teachings before, I would receive new and vital revelation from these teachers. I immediately made a quality decision **always to have an open heart to receive God's Word.** I believe we can receive from **any** minister who is preaching from God's Word — if we decide to.

Moffatt's translation of James 1:21 says, *"Make a soil*

in your heart of humble modesty for the Word." Be good soil! Break up the hard ground!

4. James 3:13 says, *"Who is a wise man and endued with knowledge among you? Let him shew out of a good conversation his works with meekness of wisdom."* Dakes Reference Bible says that true wisdom always is accompanied with meekness and gentleness. Proud, overbearing, and disdainful men may pass as scholars and may have learning, but what they have is not true wisdom.

God's Promises to the Meek

"The meek will he guide in judgment: and the meek will he teach his way" (Psalm 25:9). God will guide and teach the meek. God will guide you with His eye. If you are beholding His face through His Word and in prayer daily, He can guide you more easily. But if you're not beholding His face, He could be trying to direct you with His eyes, but you won't be able to see it or receive it. He cannot and will not guide where pride and arrogance reside.

Matthew 5:5 says, *"Blessed are the meek: for they shall inherit the earth."* It is the meek person of God who will prosper in every area of life.

"The meek shall eat and be satisfied: they shall praise the Lord that seek him: your heart shall live for ever" (Psalm 22:26). God gives contentment to the person who allows the fruit of meekness to live big within him, because the meek person totally depends upon God!

10
Self-Control

The Scripture tells us in Hebrews 4:15 that Jesus was "tempted in all points like as we are, yet without sin." In the four Gospels, it is recorded that Jesus was led up of the Spirit into the wilderness to be tempted of the devil. He was tempted in the three areas of sin most common to man since the fall of Adam: the lust of the flesh, the lust of the eyes, and the pride of life. Jesus overcame all of these areas of temptation by speaking the Word of God.

By resisting Satan with the spoken Word, Scripture records that the devil left Him and Jesus returned in the power of the Spirit. Jesus exercised restraint over His own impulses, emotions, and desires.

Webster defines self-control as "restraint exercised over one's own impulses, emotions, or desires." Self-control in the Greek means "inward strength, to be strong or powerful."

Training for Excellence in "Self-Control"

Paul recognized that every Christian must exercise this same inward strength if he is to run the race successfully. *"Do you not know that in a race all the runners compete, but [only] one receives the prize? So run [your race] that you may lay hold [of the prize] and make it yours"* (1 Corinthians 9:24, AMPLIFIED).

Paul was making a comparison between the Olympic games of his day and the spiritual race of the Christian. In an Olympic game, only one could receive the prize. In the race God has set before us, we are all eligible to win! We are not competing against **each other**, but we are running (competing) against the devil. How sad it is that in the Body of Christ some groups have tried to compete against each other. This is not God's way, brothers and sisters in the Lord, for God desires that we be a strength one to another, thereby building up His entire Body.

Paul wants us to envision an actual race so we will press toward the mark for the prize of the high calling of God in Christ Jesus (Philippians 3:14) What Paul is saying is that we must have the same compelling determination for highest excellence as a Christian as the Olympic athlete has for his endeavors. It is not enough to be an "average Christian." Paul exhorts us to be "above average." He exhorts us to seek excellence. This excellence can be achieved only through self-control.

First Corinthians 9:25 says, *"And every man that striveth for the mastery is temperate (self-controlled)* **in all things**.... *"* An athlete in training must exercise a great deal of discipline to excel. His training will include physical workouts, proper diet, and adequate rest. This same discipline must be applied to the Christian's life.

Your spirit man can be exercised through prayer and application of God's Word. Speaking God's Word (applying it to your life) creates an atmosphere of control. In other words, you can control your life and can resist the temptations of the devil by the words that you speak. This is why Jesus spoke God's Word in the wilderness. By speaking God's Word, He was able to control Himself and overcome the devil at the same time.

As you walk through life, you will have ample opportunity (as Jesus did) to let your spirit man dominate your emotions and desires. When we are offended or disappointed by others, our natural tendency is to respond in anger. When we explode in anger, we are not being controlled by our spirit man but by emotions and impulses.

A fellow once said, "I have no trouble walking with God in the Christian life. It's just all the other Christians that I have problems with!" That sounds funny, but that's really the way some people feel. In becoming a part of the family of God, we must learn to live together as family. God can use other brothers and sisters in the Lord to develop fruit in our lives if we allow Him to.

"He that is slow to anger is better than the mighty; and he that ruleth his spirit than he that taketh a city" (Proverbs 16:32). It is important to keep your emotions under control. As you pray in the Spirit, you will be calmed down and will build up your spirit man to take control over your feelings. Do not give place to the devil. *"Be ye angry, and sin not: let not the sun go down upon your wrath"* (Ephesians 4:26).

Righteous anger is a godly emotion expressed against sin. (Jesus showed divine anger toward the money changers in the Temple.) However, it is extremely important that you do not confuse human anger with godly anger. Some people have tried to cover up their personal anger, excusing it as righteous indignation when, in actuality, it is the wrath of man as listed in James 1:19 and 20. *"Understand [this], my beloved brethren. Let every man be quick to hear, (a ready listener,) slow to speak, slow to take offense and to get angry. For man's anger does not promote the righteousness God [wishes and requires]"* (AMPLIFIED). God wants all of His children, including you and me, to learn self-control in their emotions as well as their bodies.

We mentioned earlier that the tongue is to be used to create an atmosphere of positive control, but it also can be used as a negative force if it is not brought under the control of the Holy Spirit. James says that the tongue is like a bit in a horse's mouth or like the small helm of a ship. The bit controls the movement of the horse; the helm controls the course of the ship (see James 3:1-10).

The tongue, although a very small member of the body, controls, directs, and sets the course for the body. If the tongue is left without control, it is a *"world of iniquity and is set on fire of hell"* (James 3:6). Like a fire, it can destroy. Man without God has a tendency to use his tongue for gossip, criticism, and backbiting. Some Christians also have been guilty of using their tongue as a destructive force, because they have lacked control of their tongue.

I would like to use a simple comparison of an orange and a lemon to illustrate that *"...out of the abundance of the heart the mouth speaks"* (Matthew 12:34). Both the lemon and the orange are fruit, similar on the outside, merely different in size and color. You will notice when you squeeze them, however, that they are distinctly different, for out of the orange comes a sweet juice, while out of the lemon comes a sour juice.

Did the pressure of the squeeze cause the lemon to be sour, or did the pressure of the squeeze simply bring out what was inside the lemon? I think it is clear from this illustration that pressure doesn't make us sweet or sour; it simply brings out what's on the inside of us!

As you yield yourself to the Word of God—studying, meditating, and confessing the Scriptures—your tongue will become bridled. You will begin to speak as God would speak, bringing edification to others and ministering grace to the hearer (Ephesians 4:29).

Another area of discipline important to the well-trained athlete is proper diet. The diet of the Christian must include the Word of God. Jesus said, *"...Man shall not live by bread alone, but by every word that proceeds out of the mouth of God"* (Matthew 4:4). The strength of your spirit man depends on the daily nourishment you gain from the Bread of Life (Jesus, the Living Word). *"Thy words were found, and I did eat them; and thy word was unto me the joy and rejoicing of mine heart..."* (Jeremiah 15:16).

In the same way that you partake of the Bread of Life through your eyes and ears, you feed yourself with negative influences. If a person, for example, reads literature or watches television programs filled with lust, violence, and terror, he cannot expect to experience the peace of God on a daily basis. In computer science terms, *"garbage in—garbage out."* Another way to say it is, "You are what you eat."

Also of primary importance to the athlete in training

are times of rest and refreshing. Likewise, the Christian needs times of rest and refreshing. *"For with stammering lips and another tongue will he speak to this people. To whom he said, this is the rest wherewith ye may cause the weary to rest..."* (Isaiah 28:11,12).

There is truly a rest and a refreshing when you take time in your busy schedule to pray in the Spirit. You must never grow weary in well doing. It will take self-control to discipline yourself to take a daily time for prayer. Just as an athlete receives strength through rest, you also will receive strength through prayer and through quiet time communing with the Father.

At other times, just a break from the day-to-day routine (a quiet walk, a drive in the country, or even an afternoon of fishing) will cause a refreshing to come to you. In the word "recreation" we see the word "recreate." In taking time for leisure, creativity is aroused within one's heart and mind. I have found in times like these, I can more readily hear the creative thoughts of God concerning my family and the ministry.

In 1 Corinthians 9:26, Paul goes on to say that an athlete should not run uncertainly, aimlessly, or without an end goal. He also said in Philippians 3:13 that he did not consider himself to have already attained perfection (maturity), but he was pressing on toward the mark (goal) for the prize of God's heavenly calling in Christ Jesus. Taylor's Version says, *"I strained to reach the end of the race."* We must not stop and become complacent at any point of growth; we must press forward.

In Paul's pressing forward, he realized that he could never think upon the past ground he had already covered. An athlete must forget the ground he already has covered in a race. And time is too precious for Christians to waste in condemning themselves over the past. Instead, you must reach forth as an athlete—straining every nerve, muscle, and ounce of energy to come to spiritual maturity.

The key to the Christian's training is keeping his eyes fixed upon Jesus. The athlete must pursue the white line on the track. He cannot be distracted by looking to the left or to the right to keep his balance and speed. As a child of God, neither can you afford to be distracted by the tricks of the devil. Press on toward the mark of the prize of the high calling of God in Christ Jesus (Philippians 3:14).

In bringing your body under the subjection of your spirit man, don't fight as one who beats the air striking without an adversary. Our adversary is the devil—the god of this world—and our flesh is subject to the dictates of the world until it has been trained to be in subjection to the Holy Spirit, who dominates the Christian's spirit. Paul said he kept his body under because he realized he was still human. He didn't have his glorified body yet. He recognized that if he didn't keep his physical body under the control of his spirit man, it could well disqualify his witness.

Sometimes in the race of life you get knocked down, either by other Christians or by those around you. The tendency is to stay down, accepting defeat. But when you are knocked down, get up again quickly, and run with all of your might. Push past the point where human ability alone keeps you going. Push yourself into the realm of the supernatural power of God which can plummet you across the finish line and make you a winner! That's the kind of Christian God is going to use to win the world to Christ. The person who falls down and stays down is not going to be effective. Determine in your heart today that **nothing,** but **nothing** is going to hold you back from obtaining your incorruptible crown!

And then remember, you are not only in a race, but you are also in a battle. There are fleshly lusts that are warring against your soul. *"Beloved, I implore you as sojourners, strangers and exiles [in this world] to abstain from the sensual urges—the evil desires, the passions of the flesh [your lower nature]—that wage war against your soul"* (1 Peter 2:11, AMPLIFIED).

"So, since Christ suffered in the flesh [for us, for you], arm yourselves with the same thought and purpose [patiently to suffer rather than fail to please God]. For whoever has suffered in the flesh [having the mind of Christ] has done with [intentional] sin—has stopped pleasing himself and the world, and pleases God. So that he can no longer spend the rest of his natural life living by [his] human appetites and desires, but [he lives] for what God wills" (1 Peter 4:1,2, AMPLIFIED).

"I appeal to you therefore, brethren, and beg of you in view of [all] the mercies of God, to make a decisive dedication of your bodies—presenting all your members and faculties—as a living sacrifice, holy (devoted, consecrated) and well pleasing to God, which is your

reasonable (rational, intelligent) service and spiritual wor-
ship. Do not be conformed to this world—this age, fashion-
ed after and adapted to its external, superficial customs.
But be transformed (changed) by the [entire] renewal of
your mind—by its new ideals and its new attitude—so that
you may prove [for yourselves] what is the good and accept-
able and perfect will of God, even the thing which is good
and acceptable and perfect [in His sight for you]" (Romans
12:1,2, AMPLIFIED).

Aids to Developing Self-Control
(Fighting the Good Fight)

1. **The Word of God is your sword!** *"And take the*
helmet of salvation and the sword the Spirit wields, which
is the Word of God" (Ephesians 6:17, AMPLIFIED).

2. **Cast down imaginations.** *"(For the weapons of our*
warfare are not carnal, but mighty through God to the pull-
ing down of strong holds;) Casting down imaginations, and
every high thing that exalteth itself against the knowledge
of God, and bringing into captivity every thought to the
obedience of Christ" (2 Corinthains 10:4,5).

3. **Do not be entangled with the distractions of this**
life! *"No man that warreth entangleth himself with the af-*
fairs of this life; that he may please him who hath chosen
him to be a soldier" (2 Timothy 2:4).

4. **Put on the whole armour of God, and pray**
always in the Spirit. *"Put on the whole armour of God,*
that ye may be able to stand against the wiles of the devil.
For we wrestle not against flesh and blood, but against

principalities, against powers, against the rulers of the darkness of this world, against spiritual wickedness in high places. Wherefore take unto you the whole armour of God, that ye may be able to withstand in the evil day, and having done all, to stand. Stand therefore, having your loins girt about with truth, and having on the breastplate of righteousness; And your feet shod with the preparation of the gospel of peace; Above all, taking the shield of faith, wherewith ye shall be able to quench all the fiery darts of the wicked. And take the helmet of salvation, and the sword of the Spirit, which is the word of God: Praying always with all prayer and supplication in the Spirit, and watching thereunto with all perseverance and supplication for all saints" (Ephesians 6:11-18).

11
Gifts Bearing Fruit

In my earlier years as a Christian, I received a lot of teaching on the fruit of the Spirit, but little teaching or demonstration on the gifts of the Spirit. However, in studying the Scriptures, I have found that God desires that His children flow in both the gifts of the Spirit **and** the fruit of the Spirit.

Some people interpret 1 Corinthians 12 to mean that Paul is saying the supernatural gifts of the Spirit are not necessary for today, that we need only to operate in love. This is not what Paul is saying.

After explaining the supernatural operation of the gifts of the Spirit, Paul was emphasizing that these gifts need to be operated in love, love being the "more excellent way" of which Paul speaks. Paul said in 1 Corinthians 14:1, *"Follow after charity (love), and desire spiritual gifts...."*

Paul was setting forth an Old Testament principle in the Corinthian letters. This can be seen in the type and shadow of the priestly robes. In the Book of Exodus, God told Moses to build a tabernacle in which He could dwell. He told Moses to appoint priests who would minister to Him within the tabernacle.

The priests were to wear robes with hems lined with alternating pomegranate fruit and golden bells. The bells were necessary to let the people outside the tabernacle know the priest was still alive and that his offering was acceptable to God. It also was important for the people to know where he was ministering within. The pomegranates were to soften the noise of the bells.

The bells represent the gifts of the Spirit, while the pomegranates represent the fruit of the Spirit. We need a balance of both the gifts and the fruit operating in our lives.

Paul tried to emphasize this balance as he referred to the gifts of the Spirit. Paul was not saying that we do not need the gifts of the Spirit—only that **love should be our chief aim.** He was showing us that love would cause the gifts to flow in their proper order and demonstration to meet people's needs. We see this balance demonstrated in the life of Jesus, and we should follow in His footsteps. Jesus operated in excellency of ministry, and the key to His excellence was His love and compassion for the people.

The fruit of the Spirit always must accompany the supernatural manifestations of the Spirit. *"If I [can] speak in the tongues of men and [even] of angels, but have not love [that reasoning, intentional, spiritual devotion such as is inspired by God's love for and in us], I am only a noisy gong or a clanging cymbal"* (1 Corinthians 13:1, AMPLIFIED). People who do not operate in the fruit of the Spirit along with the gifts of the Spirit are often offensive to others.

Some Christians who have operated in the gifts of the Spirit have neither flowed in the love of God, nor have they used self-control in certain situations. This has offended other believers in the Body of Christ. In fact, it has brought about a negative attitude toward the supernatural workings of the Spirit in some cases.

In operating in the gifts of the Spirit, it is important to learn self-control. First Corinthians 14:32 says, *"And the spirits of the prophets are subject to the prophets."* In some services, I have had people tell me they couldn't hold back the gift. But you **can** hold the gift, and sometimes you may **need** to do so for the benefit of order and peace in a service. *"For God is not the author of confusion, but of peace..."* (1 Corinthians 14:33). And the Spirit of God further admonishes us, *"Let all things be done decently and in order"* (1 Corinthians 14:40).

There will be times in a service or meeting when more than one person will have a tongue and interpretation, but only one is to speak. In such times, be very sensitive to those in authority, allowing them to speak first. Self-control in holding your own tongue is developed as you submit to those in authority (leadership) over that particular service.

There may be times when you have a supernatural word from the Lord, but it may be for you personally rather than for the entire congregation. There may be other times when God will give you a word for someone else. Before giving your word, as a point of being sensitive to the Spirit of God, pray first, asking the Lord for whom the particular word is intended. You many need to go to someone to deliver the word personally or, if it is for the entire congregation, trust the Spirit of God to speak to the leadership. They either will be given the same word you have been given, or the Spirit of God will ask them to call upon you to give it. Also, it may not be the time that God desires it to be spoken forth. Sometimes words are given that are to be shared later.

In all of this, we must ask ourselves, "What is my motivation?" Some people enjoy listening to themselves speak! Some people just want to be heard by others or be recognized. Some have a spirit of pride, thinking that God can only use them to bring forth what needs to be said. Sometimes prophecies are simply people giving forth the desires of their own heart rather than God speaking to the people. Take time to "learn of Him"—Jesus. Let Him direct You. **Trust the Spirit of God!** He won't fail! And in doing so, you will be a contributor to peace and order!

12
Abiding in the Vine

"Abide in me, and I in you. As the branch cannot bear fruit of itself, except it abide in the vine; no more can ye, except ye abide in me" (John 15:4). The Amplified translation of this verse says, *"Dwell in Me and I will dwell in you.—Live in Me and I will live in you. Just as no branch can bear fruit of itself without abiding in (vitally united to) the vine, neither can you bear fruit unless you abide in Me."*

To abide means "to continue in a place, to remain stable or fixed in a state, to endure without yielding, withstand, to conform to, and to stay."

Jesus said in John 8:31, *"...If you abide in My Word—hold fast to My teachings and live in accordance with them—you are truly My disciples"* (AMPLIFIED). There is a definite difference in being a believer in Christ Jesus and being a disciple of Christ Jesus. First John 2:6 says, *"Whoever says he abides in Him ought—as a personal debt—to walk and conduct himself in the same way in which He walked and conducted Himself"* (AMPLIFIED). You see, a disciple is one who **abides** and **continues** in the doctrine and lifestyle of his Master or Teacher—Jesus!

Many people who truly have had a born-again experience have failed to go on to be a disciple of the Lord. The same was true in Jesus' day. In the sixth chapter of John, Jesus talked to the multitudes about His being the

Bread of Life. He spoke in terms which they did not understand, and *"From that time many of his disciples went back, and walked no more with him"* (John 6:66).

The twelve disciples remained, even though they did not understand what Jesus was saying. They did realize, however, that Jesus had the words of life. And although you may not fully understand the Word of God, continue diligently in the Word and you will come to a knowledge of the truth and thereby walk in total freedom.

Those who remained with Jesus became conformed to His image. Romans 12:2 exhorts us, *"And be not conformed to this world: but be ye transformed by the renewing of your mind (with the Word of God), that ye may prove what is that good, and acceptable, and perfect, will of God."*

An amazing thing to note here is that the branches which grow on a grapevine begin to look like the vine itself. Likewise, as you and I (the branches) continue to grow in Jesus (the Vine), we will begin to look more and more like Jesus!

I remember a deeply moving story that vividly illustrates this truth. A little boy was standing in a subway station holding a boxed jigsaw puzzle. A businessman came running through the subway station trying to catch the last train that would get him to work on time. As he ran past the little boy, he accidentally knocked the box containing the puzzle out of his hands, scattering the pieces all over the concrete floor.

The hurrying executive stopped, quickly scanned the

little boy's face, the scattered puzzle pieces, and his train, which was slowly pulling out of the station. He had to make a fast decision—whether to be late for his job or to assist the startled little boy. He put his briefcase down and began to retrieve the puzzle pieces for the boy.

The little boy lifted his eyes from the box as the man dropped in a few pieces and asked, "Mister, are you Jesus?"

What a high recognition! Wouldn't we all like to have this said of us? All it takes is being consciously aware of who lives inside of us and then making every effort to allow the Spirit of God to flow through us continually.

You and I, the branches, are extensions of the Vine. The branches of themselves cannot produce fruit. They must be connected to the Vine. And the Vine is the Source of life; the branches simply bear the fruit. Mary, the mother of Jesus, did not produce Jesus; she was simply the vessel who carried Jesus and then bore Him out to the world. Likewise, we are vessels of God, carrying Jesus and bearing Him out to the world. As we abide in the Word of God, we will be more sensitive in expressing the nature of Jesus to others.

As you meditate in God's Word, allow it to dwell in you richly, for then sin cannot remain in your life. *"**No one who abides in Him**—who lives and remains in communion with and in obedience to Him, **[deliberately and knowingly] habitually commits (practices) sin.** No one who habitually sins has either seen or known Him—recognized, perceived or understood Him, or has had an experimental acquaintance with Him"* (1 John 3:6, AMPLIFIED).

Purpose in your heart to let God's Word dwell in you richly **at all times.** As you face difficult situations, continue in God's Word, for some of the richest, most abundant fruit has come forth from God's people at such times. *"Let the word [spoken by] the Christ, the Messiah, have its home (in your hearts and minds) and dwell in you in [all its] richness, as you teach and admonish and train one another in all insight and intelligence and wisdom..."* (Colossians 3:16, AMPLIFIED).

The Father will be glorified as you bear much fruit. This simply means that He will not be glorified so much when we bear only small portions of fruit or irregular harvests of fruit. People will see Christ through the abundance of fruit in your life, and your heavenly Father will be glorified.

And the fruit orchards which have produced abundant crops over the years are the ones which have been well cultivated, cared for, and fertilized. These orchards have fed many with their regular harvests. As you and I allow God, the Husbandman, to cultivate and fertilize us with His Spirit and His Word, we will feed many who are hungry for the fruit of His Spirit.

Benefits of Abiding in the Vine .

A few of the benefits of abiding in the Vine (Jesus Christ) include:

1. We will be called His disciples. *"Herein is my Father glorified, that ye bear much fruit; so shall ye be my*

disciples" (John 15:8).

2. We shall ask what we will, and it shall be done. *"If ye abide in me, and my words abide in you, ye shall ask what ye will, and it shall be done unto you"* (John 15:7). To abide in God's Word is to delight yourself in His Word. *"Delight thyself also in the Lord; and he shall give thee the desires of thine heart"* (Psalm 37:4). The more we delight and abide in God's Word, the more His desires will be created within us. Then we will pray according to His will (according to His Word). *"And this is the confidence that we have in him, that if we ask any thing according to his will, he heareth us: And if we know that he hear us, whatsoever we ask, we know that we have the petitions that we desired of him"* (1 John 5:14,15).

3. Christ's joy will remain in us in fullness! *"These things have I spoken unto you, that my joy might remain in you, and that your joy might be full"* (John 15:11).

4. Jesus no longer will call me a servant, but a friend! *"Henceforth I call you not servants; for the servant knoweth not what his lord doeth: but I have called you friends; for all things I have heard of my Father I have made known unto you"* (John 15:15).

5. We will be chosen of Him! *"Ye have not chosen me, but I have chosen you, and ordained you, that ye should go and bring forth fruit, and that your fruit should remain: that whatsoever ye shall ask of the Father in my name, he may give it you"* (John 15:16).

When we abide in Him, we will not be barren or unfruitful but abounding in the knowledge of our Lord Jesus

Christ. Abiding in the Vine is walking in the Spirit, and the results are **a fruitful life!**

A FRUITFUL LIFE . . . WALKING IN THE SPIRIT

	FRUIT	FRUIT ROBBERS	INSECTICIDE
●	Self-Control	Wrong Thoughts	II Corinthians 10:4,5
●	Peace	Worry	Philippians 4:6
●	Joy	Discouragement	I Samuel 30:6
●	Peace	Guilt	Romans 8:1
●	Peace	Confusion	II Timothy 1:7
●	Peace	Fear	I John 4:18, II Timothy 1:7
●	Love	Unforgiveness	Matthew 18:21,22
●	Love	Bitterness	Hebrews 12:15
●	Love	Envy	James 3:16
●	Peace	Strife	James 3:16
●	Love	Selfishness	I Corinthians 13:5, Philippians 2:4
●	Meekness	Pride	Proverbs 16:18, Philippians 2:3, James 4:6
●	Self-Control	Excessiveness	I Corinthians 9:25
●	Faithfulness	Slothfulness	Hebrews 6:12
●	Self-Control	Critical Tongue, Gossiping	Ephesians 4:29, I Peter 3:10
●	Self-Control	Anger	James 1:19,20
●	Patience	Impatience	I Corinthians 13:4
●	Gentleness	Harshness, Violence	II Timothy 2:24
●	Self-Control	Immorality	I Corinthians 6:18

112

13
Fruit Robbers

The diagram on the opposite page reveals fruit robbers which try to destroy or damage the fruit of our lives as Christians.

John 10:10 says the thief comes but to steal, kill, and destroy. The Word of God acts as a powerful insecticide which wards off pests that would try to rob the fruit from the vine or tree. Hebrews 4:12 says God's Word is *"quick and powerful"* against any fruit robbers.

Fruit	Fruit Robbers
PEACE	*Worry or care or anxiety* - *"Be careful for nothing; but in everything by prayer and supplication with thanksgiving let your requests be made known unto God"* (Philippians 4:6).
JOY	*Discouragement* - In 1 Samuel 30:6, David encouraged himself in the Lord. *"And David was greatly distressed; for the people spake of stoning him, because the soul of all the people was grieved, every man for his sons and for his daughters: but David*

encouraged himself in the Lord his God."

JOY & PEACE **Guilt or Condemnation** - *"There is therefore now no condemnation to them which are in Christ Jesus, who walk not after the flesh, but after the Spirit"* (Romans 8:1).

PEACE **Confusion or Fear** - *"For God hath not given us the spirit of fear; but of power, and of love, and of a sound mind"* (2 Timothy 1:7).

"There is no fear in love; but perfect love casteth out fear: because fear hath torment. He that feareth is not made perfect in love (1 John 4:18).

"The Lord is my light and my salvation; whom shall I fear? the Lord is the strength of my life; of whom shall I be afraid?" (Psalm 27:1).

LOVE **Unforgiveness** - *"And when ye stand praying, forgive if ye have ought against any: that your Father also which is in heaven may forgive you your trespasses"* (Mark 11:25).

114

> *"Then came Peter to him (Jesus) and said, Lord, how oft shall my brother sin against me, and I forgive him? till seven times? Jesus saith unto him, I say not unto thee, Until seven times: but, Until seventy times seven"* (Matthew 18:21,22).

LOVE **Bitterness** - *"Looking diligently lest any man fail of the grace of God; lest any root of bitterness springing up trouble you, and thereby many be defiled"* (Hebrews 12:15).

LOVE **Jealousy and envy** - *"For where envying and strife is, there is confusion and every evil work"* (James 3:16).

"Charity [love] suffereth long, and is kind; charity envieth not; charity vaunteth not itself, is not puffed up" (1 Corinthians 13:4).

PEACE **Strife** - *"For where envying and strife is, there is confusion and every evil work* (James 3:16).

LOVE **Self-Centeredness and Selfishness** *"Doth not behave itself unseemly, seeketh not her own, is not* *easily provoked, thinketh no evil"* (1 Corinthians 13:5).

"Look not every man on his own things, but every man also on the things of others" (Philippians 2:4).

MEEKNESS **Pride** - *"Pride goeth before destruction, and an haughty spirit before a fall"* (Proverbs 16:18).

"Let nothing be done through strife or vainglory; but in lowliness of mind let each esteem other better than themselves" (Philippians 2:3).

"...God resisteth the proud, but giveth grace unto the humble" (James 4:6).

SELF-CONTROL **Excessiveness** - *"And every man that striveth for the mastery is temperate in all things. Now they do it to obtain a corruptible crown; but we an incorruptible"* (1 Corinthians 9:25).

FAITHFULNESS **Slothfulness** - *"That ye be not slothful, but followers of them who through faith and patience inherit the promises* (Hebrews 6:12).

LOVE GOODNESS SELF-CONTROL	**Critical Tongue, Gossiping, Backbiting** - *"Let no corrupt communication proceed out of your mouth, but that which is good to the use of edifying, that it may minister grace unto the hearers"* (Ephesians 4:29). *"For he that will love life, and see good days, let him refrain his tongue from evil, and his lips that they speak no guile"* (1 Peter 3:10).
PATIENCE GENTLENESS	**Anger and Impatience** - *"Wherefore, my beloved brethren, let every man be swift to hear, slow to speak, slow to wrath: For the wrath of man worketh not the righteousness of God"* (James 1:19,20).
PATIENCE	**Impatience and Hastiness** - *"Cast not away therefore your confidence, which hath great recompence of reward. For ye have need of patience, that, after ye have done the will of God, ye might receive the promise"* (Hebrews 10:35,36).
SELF-CONTROL	**Immorality** - *"Flee fornication. Every sin that a man doeth is*

	without the body; but he that committeth fornication sinneth against his own body" (1 Corinthians 6:18).
ALL FRUITS	**Lack of Knowledge** - *"My people are destroyed for lack of knowledge..."* (Hosea 4:6).

BOOKS BY SHARON DAUGHERTY

Walking in the Spirit
A Fruitful Life

Called By His Side

**Available from your local bookstore,
or from:**

Harrison House
P. O. Box 35035
Tulsa, OK 74153

Sharon is actively involved in ministry alongside her husband, Billy Joe Daugherty, pastor of Victory Christian Center in Tulsa, Oklahoma. Sharon and her husband are both graduates of Oral Roberts University.

Anointed of God as a Psalmist, Sharon has written and recorded several albums.

Sharon is author of Walking in the Spirit — A Fruitful Life and Called By His Side. She also teaches at Victory Bible Institute, an outreach of Victory Christian Center, and is the mother of four children — Sarah, Ruth, John, and Paul.

To contact Sharon,
write:

Sharon Daugherty
Victory Christian Center
7700 S. Lewis
Tulsa, OK 74136

*Please include your prayer requests
and comments when you write.*